# Spinning
# Off
# Bukowski

# Spinning
# Off
# Bukowski

## Steve Richmond

SUN DOG PRESS
NORTHVILLE, MICHIGAN
1996

SPINNING OFF BUKOWSKI
Copyright ©1996 by Steve Richmond

Edited by Daniel Waldron

Cover design by Matthew Moroz

Front cover photo of Charles Bukowski by William Childress

Back cover photo of Steve Richmond by David Garcia

Grateful acknowledgment is made by the author for the blend of encouragement, tolerance, and vital advice given by David Garcia, Douglas Goodwin, Marvin Malone, John Martin, and Jeffrey Weinberg.

The publisher wishes to thank Judy Berlinski, Roger Jackson, and Dan Waldron for their professional help and guidance in the preparation of this book. Special thanks to Nicky Drumbolis and Michael Montfort, the keepers of the flame.

Library of Congress Cataloging-in-Publication Data

Richmond, Steve, 1941—
        Spinning off Bukowski / Steve Richmond.—1st ed.
            p.    cm.
        Includes bibliographical references and index.
        ISBN 0-941543-10-2 (paper: alk. paper).
        ISBN 0-941543-11-0 (signed paper: alk. paper).
        1. Bukowski, Charles—Biography. 2. Poets, American—
        20th century—Biography. I. Title.
        PS3552.U4Z84 1996
        811'.54—dc20
        [B]                                                        96-2076
                                                                   CIP

Printed in the United States of America

*For Poet Douglas Goodwin*

"Poetry is the reporting of truth. Do your work. Make it new."

*—Ezra Pound*

# FOREWORD

The amazing thing about Charles Bukowski is that he lived as long as he did. He was 73 when he died in 1994, and much of his life had been one long episode of dissipation and riotous living. Or at least as riotous as possible for a penniless poet whose whole existence seemed centered on booze, broads, and benders.

But through it all, Bukowski wrote. He wrote some of the most penetrating poetry and prose of our time. He wrote compulsively, and tells how in the depths of his poverty, broke, freezing, he found a pencil stub and wrote "in the margins of dirty newspapers" because nothing else was available.

Eventually, out of the alcohol haze and the abuse he heaped on his own body, out of what he himself calls "the hard and woolly crap," he rose to eminence in the literary field and to financial largess beyond his wildest dreams.

Ironically, Bukowski is probably better known outside the English-speaking world than within it. In Germany, for example, he is regarded as a major modern American poet. Independent presses, primarily John Martin's Black Sparrow Press in Santa Rosa, California, have pioneered the way; but Bukowski is yet to be taught regularly in U.S. schools and colleges, possibly because his blistering candor and astringent attitude question the very values at the root of our society.

We like our heroes to be perfect. We don't want flesh and blood; we want monuments. We demand idols—flawless, pure, and super-human. Bukowski was none of these. He was human, intensely so, and that is how he is captured here. With vivid words Steve Richmond brings Bukowski to life; and in the process tells a good deal about himself as poet and person, too.

For many years Richmond was a close friend of Bukowski. He was his buddy, drinking pal, and, as it turned out, devoted student. While others were oohing and aahing over mainstream versifiers, the ones taught in Lit courses at

Universities, Steve Richmond was finding in Bukowski the vitality, simplicity, unflinching imagery, and pitiless vision that great poetry is made of. In ways, he worshipped the man. Or was it the poet in the man? Or perhaps both? In any case, he looked upon Bukowski as a role model, a spiritual father, a teacher to whom he submitted his writing efforts for Bukowski's not-always-gentle critiques.

Richmond's adulation didn't cloud his powers of observation, however—a thing for which we should be endlessly grateful. Aside from self-reflection by Bukowski in his writings themselves, and in spite of the existence of a full-length biography, no previously published portrait of Charles Bukowski has been set down with the power, intimacy, and revelation of this one. *Spinning Off Bukowski* gives important insights into the human being who was Charles Bukowski—abundantly so—and certainly with a free-wheeling frankness that is sometimes startling.

But if Steve Richmond has provided from personal experience an embarrassment of riches in the totality of this book, he has also produced a work that is rewarding merely to dip into. It need not be read straight through—although it surely can be. It is intense stuff. It is also engrossing, bewitching, and as real as they come. Richmond's account not only gives us Bukowski with all his warts, it leaves us filled with an insatiable thirst to get on to Bukowski's poetry and prose—and to that of Bukowski's disciple: the author, Steve Richmond himself.

—*Daniel Waldron/Editor*

# FROM STEVE RICHMOND

Sunset time now, a cool breeze from the sea, and about half an hour ago Siskel of the Siskel & Ebert TV show inadvertently explained to me how I'm writing this book.

He was commenting on a British film and he stated that this film should not be held to a "linear standard" in how its storyline came across onscreen. Rather, this film's story was told in a *mosaic* and *impressionistic* style.

And that's how I feel as I'm writing what follows. My feelings and thoughts and recalls re Bukowski are often from 1985, then 1965, then 1971, within seconds of each other.

Among others, Kandinsky and Mondrian and Monet have given me th'Freedom, and Bukowski has educated me on how I can keep this Freedom and indeed enjoy it, and yes, keep my *huevos* attached to my lower torso, too.

Henry Charles Bukowski. "Hank." He told me never to hate "the woman". Thank God for him. He's always with me, and I'll be happy if this book brings him closer to you—and even if it doesn't.

*—Santa Monica, California*
*July 17, 1994*

9

One night in 1968 or 1969 Bukowski was here by himself and the two of us were quite drunk and he asked if he could sleep on the couch. Yes. He was in no condition to drive.

During this time period I often asked myself why the writer who I knew was the world's strongest and best scribe, why he of all living folks was visiting me and befriending me.

I couldn't figure it out.

I asked my brother Denny (five years older than myself and a fine surgeon), "Why is Bukowski coming over so much? What th'hell does he see in me? I mean why is he making me a friend?"

My brother, who always seemed to suddenly get a bit more serious and attentive when I mentioned the word 'Bukowski' gave me a quick and cogent answer, "He's on the edge. Does he have trouble keeping liquids down?"

"Yeah, he retches every 15 minutes or so," I said.

"Very ill alcoholics can't retain liquids. He's on the edge."

It's possible I was one of the few Hank grabbed by the hand and then ended his letters with "hold." Maybe Hank meant for me to *hold* and don't let him go over the goddamn edge.

Ah yes—Hank, right exactly where I sit now, began preparing for sleep on the old couch.

He took off his pants, and *MY GOD* he took off his

undershorts. He took off his shirt; I saw his back. His back shook me up some because of scars—*acne vulgaris* scars. It was much worse scarring than I had supposed. In fact, I hadn't known his extreme skin problems as a child were on his back too. I had known of his face covered with huge boils because I had read this in *Confessions of a Man Insane Enough To Live with Beasts* and also in several of his early poems, but I didn't know anything about his back. Horrible fucking scarring, man, I tell you, horrible vicious JOB OF TH'BIBLE epidermal massive damage. Shit, I thought, I know this man is 'real' but I didn't know he is *this real*. And then Hank put on again his sleeveless white undershirt. He moved slow in first sitting, then getting on his back, lying down now on the couch. A minute passed and he slowly got up to his feet and walked a step to a pile of newspapers and he picked up several parts of an old *L.A. Times* and he returned to the couch and again lay on his back.

I offered him clean sheets and a blanket but he said no.

All he wore was the undershirt, and I am the sort of fellow who feels uneasy in the company of a man or men who are nude. I was 17 feet away preparing for sleep on my used King-size I'd recently bought from the poet Max Schwartz for 80 dollars. I was taking secret side peeks at Hank to see how he was doing. I mean how often have you, gentle reader, had a friend over to your own cave and who you simply know for sure is Earth's best writer and who is lying on his back virtually naked and then slowly blanketing himself with old newspapers?

It was obvious he had done this many times before in his life on park benches scattered all over America.


My real dad, Abraham, hardly ever visited here and when he did he immediately, upon entering, began saying, "you should paint the walls there (gesturing at some specific wall) and move those papers away from the heater and better plaster that crack in the ceiling and put a screen on those windows and. . ."

My real pop never got drunk with me and he told me

12

being a goddamn poet is like building a house of playing cards; it will collapse and your whole life will have been a useless naive foolish WASTE OF TIME. He didn't use these words but he meant it just like TERRIBLE TRAGIC WASTE OF MY LIFE if I don't wise up quick and take the California bar test once more and pass it and join him in his probate law practice and begin doing important vital work—writing Wills for clients.

Abraham supported me all the way through UCLA Law School and once went into a terrifying red-haired man's RAGE at me when I refused his money. He was so scarlet-faced and pissed off I decided to cease yelling back at him and grab the wad in his fist and escape.

Abraham, I could tell, sometimes felt his second son was most definitely in need of Biblical sacrifice. Bukowski was my father too—FATHER OF MY ART—and now both men are dead, and thank God Bukowski, and th'gods and Abraham, too, that I am now writing from the exact spot Bukowski told me to write from: my inner gut vision.

## 2

About one year before I first met Charles Bukowski, I self-published my first book of poetry. A fellow UCLA Law School student, Stephen Malley, helped select the 30 or so poems included in *Poems by Steven Richmond.*

Malley then told me a friend of his had opened a print shop on Sunset Boulevard between Vermont and Alvarado. The shop was called Tasmania Press and Malley's friend, Don Michelle, had joined with one Al Frank to open this printshop. These two young men told me they would charge me $100 for 1000 copies. They began by setting each poem by hand, just as I had learned a bit about in Junior High School Print Shop class. What they wanted to do was print a truly gorgeous book that would show the world that Tasmania Press was a wonderful wonderful place to publish-print a book. I was there most of the dozens of hours it took Don and Al to set up my poems—letterpress printjob, offset cover, chromecoat stock—amazing grace.

A few months later I was armed with 1000 copies and I began selling copies at stores and at parties and I sent free copies to everyone I could and a few months later I'd made back about $200. ("I must have been nuts," is how I think about it aloud right now. However, being nuts did beat being a third year UCLA Law School student).

Two guys who seemed ultra-literary types—both gradu-ate students in English at UCLA—I believe they were friends of a friend—somehow I was in the same room they were in and they often spoke of their close friendship with Henry Miller. I'd just read *Tropic of Cancer* and like many others I'd instantly felt him a hero. And here are these two precious young pedants, silk scarves & all, talking about Miller like he's their very own close buddy. At first, I thought they were bullshit artists.

One day, they wrote down Henry Miller's address in Pacific Palisades. They told me that I should visit Henry Miller. I'd recently read a Miller piece in which he lamented the dozens of his fans who would camp on his front area at his cabin in Big Sur. He didn't like it at all. So I decided I would drive to his place, stick a copy of *Poems by Steven Richmond* in his mailbox, and get th'hell out of there.

About 10 A.M. one weekday morn in 1964, I drove to Miller's house and I parked on the opposite side of the street and I looked for his mailbox. Where the fuck is his mailbox? Oh shit, it's a slot in his front door. His house was a big white nice upper-middle-class wealthy person's house. The driveway was actually a large half-circle with two different exits. His front door was way off the street and I thought about it, sat in my car for awhile, getting butterflies, trying to gather courage. After all, if Henry Miller didn't get a copy of my first book of poetry, he'd never find out what a knucklehead I was.

I opened the car door, walked across the street and began walking up the 70 or so feet to his front door. And I suddenly saw Miller and another older fellow through a big arch-shaped front window. They were talking and suddenly Miller looked at me walking up to his front door and I saw him rise quick from the chair and move to his front door and he opened the door and came walking right toward me, and I stood frozen about 35 feet from the front door and he was a little old shriveled elf of a man, blue terry-cloth bath-robe on and he seemed about five feet three inches and maybe 125 pounds, and he was stooping over and 4/5 bald and about 78 years is it?—however old he was in 1964. And he came at me like who the fuck am I and what the goddamn shit am I doing?—and didn't I read his piece in a recent New Directions paperback that slammed those leech-slime idiots who bugged him up at Big Sur?

But he didn't say these things. They were in his face as

he approached, so I held my book out toward him and said something like, "Oh, I didn't want to meet you and bother you—just wanted to put this in your mailbox and go away so I wouldn't bother you. I'm sorry . . . shit!"

The ire I saw or thought I saw in his face went away, disappeared, vanished. He walked without a bit of hesitation right next to me and he took the copy of my book and he looked at the cover and he said, "This is a very good cover." (Cover etching of "Hanging" by Anna Purcell).

Then he put his right arm around my waist in a very fatherly way. He told me about those assholes who bugged him up at Big Sur. I told him I'd read his words and that's why I didn't want to bother him, just drop my book in his mailbox and get the hell away. Then he opened my book up and read some lines. He read for about four seconds and closed the book.

He was like a leprechaun, wiry and tiny and elfin, a faded middle-blue terry cloth bathrobe over pajamas, slippers, 10 A.M., it's sunny and clear and his right arm is around my waist like a kindly grandpop.

I was around 24 and six feet and about 200 pounds and muscled—I mean I was a giant man and a tiny writer, with a gigantic writer inside th'body of a little relaxed & cheerful grand-dad sprite.

I never did get to his front door. He met me half-way. He put his arm around me. Henry Miller—my Hero.

**3**

The first time I met Hank it was him in his work in a magazine called *Ole #1*. There were two poems by him in this first issue of *Ole* and I don't remember one of them and I'll never forget the other one: "freedom." That poem was the strongest poem I'd ever read up to 1965, and it's still this in 1994. Blake's little four line ode "Eternity" is as meaningful for me, but Hank's "freedom" is the most powerful ode on Earth, in my opinion.

I immediately wrote Hank a letter—his address was printed in front of *Ole #1*. I told him I felt "freedom" the strongest poem ever and I asked for his submission of work for my coming magazine *Earth #1* and I told him I was no kissy ass and I invited him to my poetry bookshop and sent him a copy of my first little self-published booklet of poems.

He responded with a kind thank-you and told me he would place it with other books various writers had been good enough to send him and he said life for him has always been fucked up and he had just returned from a trip to Santa Fe and was tired and apologized a bit because of the shortness of his letter.

I was happy to get a letter from the man who I felt had written Earth's strongest poem ever.

It's been many years since I've actually read "freedom" off a page, yet from memory: "He kept thinking of her, the way she walked and talked, and she was out again when he came back; and he knew the color of each of her dresses, and the stock and curve of each heel as well as the leg shaped by it. And she came in wearing that green dress, his favorite, filthy like a dung-eating swine, love's reek, and he took out the butcher knife and tore away the cloth before her . . ."

I remember most all of it. No reason to quote it now. I wanted to meet the man who wrote that, because I knew he wrote stronger than me and when I'd begun writing poetry several years earlier I had not read anyone I thought/felt could do this. Had I read "freedom" before I began writing poetry, it's likely I wouldn't have started writing. I felt like I was filling a gap, a vacuum, there was no one except Ginsberg alive and he was homo. Heterosexuals needed a voice and no man was doing it: *speaking for man.* Indeed a man *was* doing it and I just hadn't discovered him/his work yet. So, it pissed me off in a way. It was too late to quit writing because I'd committed and *motherfucker goose-shit* it was very disappointing to find out once again I would not be numberfuckingone.

In early 1964 I wrote my first line, "Axed forehead of yon splendorous beast . . ." This came the morning after I'd watched a French documentary film in UCLA's Business Building auditorium, *Blood of the Beasts.* It was a film about slaughterhouses and even more about lovable horses and other kind animals. The poem was terrible and I worked on it for months, day and night. When I finished with it, it was even worse. But it didn't rhyme.

I was in Law School at UCLA and the more I wrote poems the less I felt like ending up a lawyer. So when I graduated from Law School at UCLA, I happily flunked the Bar Test once, and opened a small poetry bookshop. The shop was open for business and then I ran into Hank's "freedom." It stunned me. I knew instantly he'd wipe me out if I contested him so I did the wise thing, I joined him. I didn't think and I didn't feel there was any man out there who had a bit to teach me about how to write strong verse. Creeley was from th'mind, it seemed.

18

I had sat in Jack Hirschman's Poetry Class at UCLA and I'd been exposed to Creeley's work, and works of Ginsberg, Frumkin, Hine, Dylan Thomas, Olson, Corso, McClure, and McClure was pretty strong—but he liked Hollywood and I'd been raised in Hollywood from age five to 19 and I knew Hollywood was his Achilles Heel. I checked Leroi Jones, and Jones was very strong too, but he'd just gone African-named and I knew it was Leroi Jones and not Amiri Baraka who would be dangerous in th'ring. Hemingway had recently lined up the back of his head with his wife's new drapes and we all know what happened to the drapes. Ferlinghetti? I checked his *Coney Island of the Mind* and City Lights' *Pocket Book Series Number 1*—very good. But I listened to him read his work on tape or a record album and he lisped. I didn't like lispers; I'm sorry I don't like lispers; fuck me I felt he was weak in that Russian fur hat and reading all over like a precious guru. Fuck gurus. That's a terrible word, "gurus."

I'd checked all the poets in Allen's big anthology from Grove, I believe, Perkoff and Blackburn (my favorite) and Ashbery and Olson and 30 or so others and I read every paragraph each had written about his craft in the rear of this anthology and I felt I could still write stronger than any of 'em. Why? The answer is simple. I was a knucklehead.

I didn't count on meeting up with Bukowski. I didn't believe such a volcano existed. It wasn't until my first meeting with this man in person, that I finally realized this man was as powerful as his work.

He was 44, I was 24. He could teach me, and he has.

## 4

Hank's first letter to me thanks me for mailing him my first book. It's dated March 24, 1965. His second letter is dated June 11, 1965 and is one and a half pages single spaced and the bottom half of page two is one of those wild 60's Buk mixed pen-and-colored-marker-pen illustrations.

This second letter responds to me having sent him several poems and snapshots of my own charcoal drawings. It's really my drawings, Hank writes, that make it possible for him to invite me over to his place for a very first meeting/visit. It's June of 1965, I'm graduating from UCLA Law School and he worries about me being mixed up with the law. My poetry book-shop is about to open and my chosen name for the shop, "Earth Books & Gallery," has Hank joking that I must be nuts. He includes his phone number and asks me to call if I really wish to visit. I called, though I can't remember now anything at all about my telephone talk with him.

I do remember knocking at his door at 5124 De Longpre Avenue in East Hollywood. It's about 8 P.M. and night-time and his is the court apartment nearest to the street and there is a little cement porch at his front door and the outside doorlight is turned on, about a 75 Watt bulb. It's a one story court-style group of apartments painted white and maybe constructed in the late 1920's. I'm familiar with the neighborhood because between six to 19 years old I grew up and lived two and a half miles west of his place.

I stand at his door and barely knock when he opens up and raises his eyes and face just a bit up to his right and in a very split second he has seen me. Well, his whole opening his door and welcoming me in and seeing me at first is all done relaxed, not too slow not too fast, all in one easy fluid warm welcoming motion, not *flow* but yes, sort of a single relaxed flow of unnervous motion. Obviously he's not anxious about me coming over. I'm not nervous either. I'm happy to be there. I'm visiting/meeting the man who has written poems that have me thinking nobody alive on Earth has written any better poetry, not even close. We shake hands. I think we shook hands. I'm sure we shook hands right away, but before this I remember the very first thing I saw as I entered was his quite old standard typewriter. It was on a small typing table, the sort which has a top which is hardly larger than the bottom area of his old typewriter. The typer is just to my right as I walk in. It's up against the right inner door jamb almost. It can't be more than three inches from the right side of his door as I enter. There's no chair for this typer on the small typewriter table. It's placed there, maybe for me to catch it first; yes, why not? It makes sense.

Hank is wearing a short sleeved dress shirt, Dacron wash & wear, pastel hue, buttoned in front with collar open, white Tee shirt underneath. Black or dark brown post office worker shoes, laces knotted and bowed, not too little, not too much of a shine, he's been working in those shoes (work slacks, shirt tucked under, belted, clean/neat-enough work slacks).

I can't recall if Bukowski was clean shaven or wore a thin moustache that first evening. His nose, though, is unforgettable. It took over my vision for the first ten seconds or so. "Drinker-heavy alcoholic-boy oh boy" are the words best defining my initial thoughts. Veined, huge, red, long drinker's, sot fellow's nose. It said immediately to me *I have been there and you haven't. I've lived it and you are only perhaps beginning to approach it your first time, kid. Don't fuck with me. I know you*

21

*won't by the way your eyes are right now obsessing on me. I am the point man up front. Where he goes I have been and made sure it's worthy of Bukowski ...*

I was being talked to inside me by Hank's nose and right at the end of this soliloquy my own inner voice took over, attempting to calculate in numbers just how many quarts, fifths, pints, and beers it took him to achieve a nose which speaks reams before his voice box even has to utter one word. As soon as I saw the nose I knew the man it was attached to would be my mentor. My unconscious knew this right away. My conscious mind was busy adding and multiplying an olio of various alcoholic beverage containers. Still to this day my consciousness will not fully accept Hank as my mentor without a whole list of attached conditions subsequent and conditions precedent, etc. It's too often wrong and still a stubborn son of a bitch, my consciousness.

Finally I raise my eyes a bit from Hank's nose to his eyes—luminous green, not blue at all, not anything but Lion Feline Green. Not dark nor light green. It's a rare color. I've only seen that green in human eyes a few times in my 53 years. His hair is short, brown, perhaps lightly oiled, combed straight back. His face is going to die in a month or two, so creased and lined and almost arid. He needs moisture, he needs water, he needs air, he needs something!

He needs spirit, that's what he needs. Maybe that's why I'm standing a few feet west of him now, and maybe not. I'm here to kick his ass and I don't even know it. I think I'm here to meet Earth's greatest living poet and maybe learn something. He looks so old, as if he has about two months to live.

While we're standing there in his front room, I have no knowledge of *Outsider #3* nor its contents, no knowledge of *It Catches My Heart in Its Hands*. I've read the titles of these publications a few times in various mags but I've read hundreds of titles of magazines. Had I read a copy of *Outsider #3*, it's possible I would have been too frightened/awed/intimidated to ever knock on Charles Bukowski's front door. I can see he's trying to figure me, taking my measure, he is. A bit of "What the fuck is this person?" Not who, but what, yet he's not showing me a thing body language-wise which tells me he's trying to figure me. It's in the slight angle, again, that he's holding his noggin-face-angle of his chin up to his tophead. I mean his chin is a degree or two not perfectly underneath his tophead. His face is ever so slightly leaning on his chin, his tophead a degree or two leaning to his right, my left. From his chin down he is standing straight up and down.

So he's figuring me and I know this from the stance of his head from chin up. He's looking, looking IN me, exactly I suspect as he studies horses before he bets on them.

Hey, I'm nothing but a young buck trying to beat up on a King Buk and take all the women for my own, screw'em all with my cliché seed, give all the babies my noble arrogant chin, give them my character, knock the old coot out of this tribe, I'm an animal, the most vicious species on Earth, I make H Bombs, too.

I'm not worried. Like *Mad* Magazine's Alfred E. N., "what, me worry?" Years later my pop Abe will tell me, "You love yourself far too much to ever love a woman." Abe ought to know, he writes poetry too. Always about his love of God. Well, perhaps this is what Buk sees that night, young Narcissus come to peer at my own reflection in the *sun pool of green clear fire water.* I don't think so. I think Abe was wrong about me, but I didn't argue with him. Abe once told me that I was wild, that he envied how free I was. Husbands, poor husbands.

There's a quietness about Hank's place, this night of my first visit. Just us two. I'd half expected Frances and Marina.* It's peaceful inside his cave, warm soft glow of light, no object to jar my X-ray spill th'beans vision. Hank's pad is just right. I will report to th'world he's just right, his cave is just right, he is Chosen, he is our Leader.

TRUTH AGAINST THE WORLD goes an old Druid

---

*Marina Bukowski. Daughter of Frances Smith and Charles Bukowski.

motto. It's a damn good thing I brought a sixpack of beer.

**5**

First things first, he directs me to the fridge in his kitchen. He tells me where it is and says, "Put the sixpack in the fridge and open up two and bring 'em back out, kid." (I doubt "kid" was said so soon, but I'm sure of all the words before "kid.") I did as he requested. It wasn't an order. Hell, God, I loved being there.

I go to his kitchen and open the fridge door and note two more sixpacks inside. I open two cans and bring them back out to his front room and hand him a beer. He sits on his old sofa and I in an old stuffed easy chair. I think we made a toast but can't remember. I start looking about his front room. It's about 12 feet wide and 20 feet long. Hank's sofa is against the south longer wall.

Ah these beers taste good. Everything is going fine. We have exchanged oral pleasantries and now we're both quiet and relaxed and drinking our fine cold Miller's or Hamm's. Right next to his sofa, to his left, are wooden shelves held up on both red bricks and a few cement blocks. Shelves are maybe three feet long and this setup rises about five feet high. All three shelves are packed with magazines, books, perfect bound, stitched, hundreds of them. Hank's work is published in every one of them. He began writing poetry when he was 35 and he was 35 in 1955.

I'm sitting in a sort of angle position, facing Hank but I'm closer to the short wall opposite the front door, I mean I'm about 15 feet from the front door.

A big old wooden desk such as one might see in an old post office building or business building is set against this short wall to my right. On top of this desk and along the whole back or so of this desk, Hank has placed an old wooden pigeonhole piece of office furniture. It's about three and a half feet tall and two and a half feet wide and it has about 30 pigeonholes set in three vertical rows of ten holes each. There are thinner and thicker packets of white typing papers in every pigeonhole. The top of this pigeonhole cabinet seems higher against the wall than the top of my head, since it's on the desk and the top of the desk is about two and a half feet high.

Papers and pens and paper clips, etc. are also on top of Hank's desk. It's all very very neatly organized. Immediately I can see Hank's extreme focus and self discipline, just by the way his working papers are so neat, so organized, perfect order. Hank is waging a campaign and his supplies and how he keeps them will definitely not be his undoing. He is taking over modern literature, that's all, he's taking over.

There is the H Bomb Sword and there is Hank's Pen as exemplified by his desk and pigeonhole cabinet on top of it and all those Bukowski writings and copies of submitted writings and letters to his many allies and also his typer against the opposite short wall next to his front door and on top of the little typewriter table. And don't forget Bukowski's authentic place/role in 1965 Modern American Literature, articulated a year or so earlier best by two Frenchmen (Sartre and Genet) who said, "America's best poet is Charles Bukowski." Did they really say it? I'll bet they did.

A couple feet to my left on the old rug is a barbell, maybe 50 pounds in weights overall. Hank sees me noting it and he jokes a little about his exercise routines with it. We're not talking much but we're each through about three beers. Hank gets up and moves to his bathroom, closes the door, and pisses, and several seconds later I hear muffled retch sounds. He comes

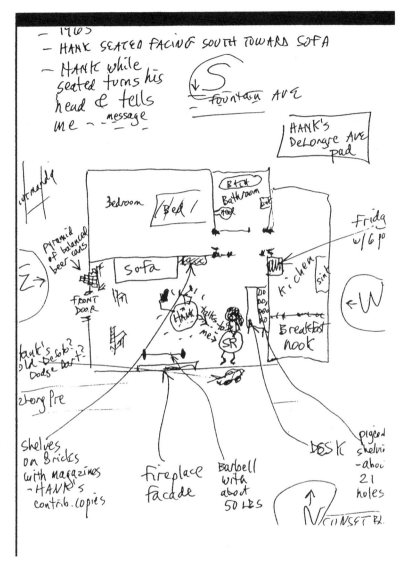

*Interior of Bukowski's De Longpre apartment. Drawing by Steve Richmond.*

out, goes right to his fridge and opens a new beer, walks back into the front room again and takes a seat on the sofa and lights his first cigar of the evening, or at least since I've arrived and looks at me and says, "You don't talk much do you?"

No, I don't talk much. What th'hell is there to say? The world's fucked up—the world's fucked up. That's all there is to say.

I didn't say this to Hank. I probably shrugged a little in the easy chair and gulped more beer.

**6**

It's about this time he pulls out my first book of poetry, the copy I mailed him three months earlier. He starts reading the very first poem:

> i tore my nails into
> my stomach ripping a hole
> big enough to put my hand
> into me with blind fingers
> feeling between intestines
> and liver for the flower of
> me, until i found it pulling
> it out, holding it in my bloody
> right hand until my left hand
> got hold of my soul, and i
> took the two and smashed them
> together until they became a
> solid piece of total beauty
> for me to throw with all
> my strength into the
> stars

I'm watching close as he reads it through. He seems not to be hurting at all so I feel it's all working nicely and then he gets to the last word and he suddenly goes, "OOOOOHHHHHH

SHIT. IT WAS GOING FINE RIGHT UP TO THAT LAST WORD—S T A R S—OHH IT'S TOO DAMN BAD—WHAT A SHAME."

I was asking myself, "What? What th'hell does he mean? Stars? What's wrong with 'stars'? Nobody's ever said anything bad about 'stars' to me in my life—hmmm."

Bukowski spoke on, "STARS is so goddamn ultra poetic. You can't use STARS. STARS STARS FUCK TH'GODDAMN STARS! What a shame, kid. You had it strong right up to the last word, then gone, ruined, all th'damn dead false sewing circle poets are forever writing STARS STARS STARS!! they can't write a line without STARS in it somewhere. I'm sorry, kid."

What he was telling me made instant sense but I tried to hedge in my mind because the 1000 copies were already printed and half the run was already distributed and there wasn't any chance I could recall every copy and have Tasmania Press change the last word of the first poem to some word, any word other than STARS.

Now it's July 11, 1994, and it's been 29 years since Hank tore his Lion's Claws into my use of STARS and I've never used the word STARS or stars or stARS even once since . . . since 10 minutes after I met Charles Bukowski, face to face.

31

**7**

1965. Hank's De Longpre digs . . . night . . . my first visit and meeting with Charles Bukowski. I'm in the cushioned easy chair looking back to my right at Hank's desk with the pigeonhole/cabinet thing he has placed on top of the desk and—this setup is something I need to make clear—the backs of each of these two pieces of office furniture . . . the backs are against the wall. His kitchen is on the opposite side of this wall. This pigeonhole cabinet is similar to any wood-enclosed book-shelves cabinet, only there are 30 pigeonholes instead of three or four wood shelves within the enclosing sides and top and bottom and the back piece of this thing is maybe . . .

Well, a year later I was in a used furniture shop and I saw the same kind of cabinet for sale and I bought it. It's in my back room right now. Three feet eight inches tall, two feet seven inches wide. Three vertical rows with ten holes each, each pigeonhole measuring (rectangles) 12 inches deep, four inches vertical width, 12 inches horizontal length. Thus reams of normal typing paper might fit easily into each opening. Why do I belabor this here? I ask you, my quite literate reader, have you ever seen such a cabinet placed on top of a big old normal heavy wooden office desk? . . . so that both the backsides of desk and cabinet are flat against a wall? Of course not, and neither had I.

It was so eye catching, this setup, that when I first walked in Hank's flat it was this desk/cabinet which I noted second, right after seeing his typer on the tiny typing table just to my right at the door, and this desk/cabinet faced me from 20 feet away, opposite wall; my main point about all this being that it was not only the uniqueness of how Hank had put the cabinet on top of the desk but also the perfect order of packets of working papers and various pens and clips and stamps and envelopes, etc., all resting on top of the desk in front of the bottom area of those pigeonholes.

I mean it was weird—I thought it was weird—because I was a 24 year old UCLA Law student who had only began writing "literature" just one year back. It would be five years more before I'd feel I'd found my own voice as a writer and here I was entering the cave/pad/studio/working quarter of a 44 year old man whom I believed/felt/*knew for sure* to be Earth's greatest strongest *living scribe*. I'd already read all other contenders: Henry Miller was still alive, Sartre, Genet, Ginsberg, and dozens of others. I'd checked every one of them, thoroughly, and it seemed to me Charles Bukowski was way way way out ahead. And now I'm a few steps inside this man's very inner sanctum and the second thing I see is a pigeonhole cabinet lifted up and placed atop a big old heavy wood office desk and it surprised me. It was the precise neatness and orderly manner in which Hank maintained every item in and on the desk/cabinet arrangement—stamps, envelopes, big envelopes, little ones, clips, color ink markers, a plastic transparent container of color drawing pens, etc. . . in direct contrast to everything else in his frontroom.

I mean this room had been straightened up, yet all the other furniture and shelves and old coffee table and chairs, etc., all were leaning one way or another, for example those three wooden shelves balanced on red bricks and two or three concrete blocks: it was about ready to topple over because his books, contributor's copies, were piled way up on one side too much and squeezed in here and leaning over the front edge of a wood shelf there, and his front room was one of those LIVED

IN HAPPY CROOKED MESSY WHO CARES CLEAN ENOUGH but just simply very unneat, thank God. It all made me very comfortable because who wants to walk into an anal front room? There was plenty of color—for I've walked into front rooms with only black and white chairs, rugs, tables, etc. Everything only in black and white, pure neurotic—*but not here in Hank's front room.*

My first thought about the contrast between his spotless/ultra neat writing area and objects and all the rest of his carefree/disorderly front room area was that it seemed very clear Hank took his work completely *serious* and with utter discipline/focus/self discipline/no nonsense/pen "at the ready" every second/every contingency planned for in advance/no room for failure.

Anal? I confess, that thought went through me too. Make sure every single visible speck of shit is out of the way, wiped away and flushed lest it somehow get in the works and foul up Charles Bukowski's performance, even 1/1000th of a percentile off absolute *perfection of firing power and bull's pupil of th'bullseye accuracy.*

In other words, *Laugh Literary And Man the Humping Guns.*

I occasionally think on Charles Baudelaire in the sense how pleasant it might be to read about him, written perhaps by a younger man, two decades younger, who had spent some time visiting and being visited by Baudelaire, this book describing in greater detail Baudelaire's desk, etc.

I've read somewhere Baudelaire planned his own reading, a public reading in Brussels, I believe. He was 43 at the time and he made sure circulars were spread throughout the area so that his following would be notified and attend and a memorable evening would result for all concerned. Eight people showed up.

It was Baudelaire's *Intimate Journals* that worked best for me. Sentences like, "The more a man gives to his art, the less he fornicates." During that first 1965 visit to Buk's De Longpre place, he told me he hadn't been laid for four years.

We kept drinking beers for hours. Somehow Bukowski had moved off his sofa to that old easy chair I'd been sitting in, and he was right in the middle of his front room, seated, and began to read one of his poems. He'd opened one of his books or mags and started reading aloud. He read four or five lines—he'd put on reading glasses just before beginning—he hadn't given me any warning or notice he was about to do this—and I was thinking to myself:

1)  this world's greatest poet is granting me my
    own  private reading of his work.

2)  I wonder why he's doing this?

3)  what were those lines he just read?

I was pretty beer high and suddenly having lines of poetry read
to me aloud and without warning. Well, I missed his first few
lines. They were blurred—not that he didn't read very
clearly—but my body & mind were alcohol fogged, *thuddy*,
socked in, you know? And so I missed his first lines and after he
read several more lines he stopped and turned his face a little
left—somehow I was now seated near his front door on a
wooden stool, or hard metal or wood folding chair of some kind.
He looked sideways at me—maybe he turned a bit right instead
of left—definitely he turned his face sideways and looked at me
and he grinned a little, and said, "Ohh you don't like this do
you?" and he set the publication down in his lap or put it on the
coffee table and said something about how he didn't enjoy
hearing poets read their own work to him, either.
        Then it came to me why he had done this: he figured I
was losing a bit of interest, getting somewhat itchy for something unique, needed a little perk-up. And so he decided to read
aloud from his work, and within a minute or so he checked me
out and realized he had figured me wrong. I was just sitting
there, courteous and quiet and respectful, it seemed to me. It
must have been on my face, my real feelings, that I detest being
with someone in a room, maybe several others, and having any
one of them read aloud his or her poetry.
        About 10 times a year I find myself imposing my own
words, me reading aloud Richmond, but never anywhere other
than in my own cave. Well, that's exactly what Hank was doing.
I was in his cave. But Hank noted I didn't enjoy it and he
stopped. I could see for a split second a look on his face which

36

told me he was thinking to himself something like,

> ". . .eh shit the kid doesn't enjoy me reading me
> so what the hell should I do now? He looks bored
> and he is boring so what can I do now to enjoy
> myself since he looks pale beyond redemption. . ."

Maybe one and a half seconds I noted this feeling in his face and also in his upper body, neck and shoulders and turning a little chest and then it left him. On the other hand, he seemed relieved somewhat he wouldn't have to "entertain me" in this manner.

Then he went to pee and retch again.

# 9

Bukowski and I took three different liquor store runs that night. We would buy two sixpacks and our second run it was I who treated. I think that night started about 8 P.M. and ended around 3 A.M. Drinking partners. We were drinking buddies that first night.

My car was a two-door Chevy II red wagon. I'm almost certain it was I who drove us to a liquor store. He directed me north a block to Sunset Boulevard and east a few blocks to Hobart Street, I believe it was. This was his number one liquor store. I remember us exiting my car and walking in and Bukowski immediately talking with the man behind the counter. Bukowski waved me off when I made a timid attempt to chip in for two more sixpacks. Right at this instant he was like a father. He became a father, taking care of expenses for a semi-son. That's how I felt. I think he sort of felt this too but he wasn't thinking about it. He was taking care of serious business, buying necessary beer. He gabbed a bit with the store keeper and he was definitely liked in this store. The talk was uphearted and familiar banter between a very good customer and a store—liquor store—man.

Odd that I so clearly remember the liquor store being on the south side of Sunset Boulevard, that I remember distinctly the time being about 9:30 to 10:00 P.M. and the street lights and dark navy blue night-time and he and I getting out of my car and walking on in the place. He's in charge, he's the leader, he's full of purpose and gusto and not a single speck of shrinking violet in him. He's Leo, he's th'Sun-Julius Caesar-King Lion—a setup for Cassius and Brutus and those sorts of back knifers because his *TRUE GRAND STYLE MAKES THEM CRINGE WITH VIRAL JEALOUSY/FILTH.*

Style—Gregarious Autocratic Beautiful Glowing Style. Am I Mark Anthony? Hmmmm?

In the store he's my father and I know what it's like to be with a father because my real father Abraham has acted just like this when I've been with him on fishing trips to th'High Sierras, and he takes me into a fishing supplies shop-sporting goods store maybe in Lone Pine and/or Bishop on our way to Convict Lake for Rainbow Speckled and Cut-throat trout. My dad Abraham is in charge in those sporting-goods shops picking number ten hooks and three lb. leader, etc.

Two Pops. Beginning at the liquor store I've suddenly got *two pops*: one for my Spirit (Hank), one for my Bank Account (Abe).

Lucky me. I mean it. Very lucky me.

We mostly sat and drank beer after beer. I didn't talk much at all because he was wise, a true sage, and I wanted to hear him, not me. He began selecting various copies of books and magazines that featured his work and one by one signed and handed them to me as gifts.

Now he gets up and walks to his head for a leak, or his kitchen for another Miller's. I'm sure we're drinking Miller's. There will be no Miller's Light for another decade or longer. He walks back into his front room. Before he sits again he goes into a bit of a boxer's crouch. Just part way though, not a full crouch. He subtly raises the topic of Creeley and Olson. He says something that is a slight put-down of Creeley/Olson. Immediately he raises his face in a quick glance my way, as if to see my reaction to his quite moderate criticism of Creeley/Olson.

I mention Creeley's *The Island*, a novel I'd read about

one year earlier. I told Hank that I liked this novel. Hank's face is not glancing at me now. His face has returned to a thought reflecting expression. Hank isn't looking at anything in particular. He's thinking, relaxed, wise, eyes almost closed, face directed a little downward and to my side. It's a wonderful shot for me. I mean like a camera, his face is beautiful, particularly in that soft glow of low to moderate lamplight. I'm catching the greatest literature maker on Earth in relaxed contemplation. I'm not flattering him, he's dead now, why should I flatter him now? To make myself larger? It's possible. To me now, 1965 then, he hasn't changed in so far as he's Earth's finest literary communicator. That's fact. Not flattery. Not me going gaga over Hank. Take it or leave it—you will anyway.

Pardon me, it's better I describe like a witness under oath, rather than pontificate like a lawyer paid to horseshit. 1965—his three-quarter profile in orange gold shadow—*alive*—there's th'word I've been seeking. He's *alive*, thinking a bit, amused in his reflections, contemplations, musings, now about Creeley/Olson and just how much I'm a believer in those fellows and their works. He's checking me out if I've gone over to Creeley/Olson, Creeley really. Creeley is Hank's real competing suitor for th'brass ring . . . *If I've gone too far over for Creely, then Hank has no choice but to forego paying for the next two sixpacks.* I'm no fool. It's been a minute since any talk so I let go, "Eh Creeley, he's a condescending prig. Yeah I liked *The Island* but only because I actually finished reading it."

Hank looked at me now. He studied me, eyed deeper into my visage. Was I conning him? That's how he looked at me. Then he said, "Let's go," and we were off to the liquor store again. Maybe the store was up on Hollywood Boulevard instead of Sunset. We were both drunk. I think he drove this time. He drove slow, took side streets skirting the Hollywood Freeway. Yes, the liquor store was on Hollywood Boulevard and Hobart Street. The southwest corner. On the drive back to his place the

40

streets were very dark. He drove very slow, very safely.

There was a phone call—it was Curtis Zahn calling. Zahn lived in the Malibu Colony. A year earlier New Directions Press published a collection of Zahn's short stories. I remember trying to read them. I couldn't get into his tales. His writing style seemed rather entangled to me and there wasn't room for me to squeeze in, find a comfortable spot to relax, stretch out, read his inner gut vision. There wasn't an inner gut vision at all, his mind was writing, it seemed to me. Cerebral web strands, thin. Anyhow every second or fourth Tuesday, I think Tuesday, Zahn hosted a *literary workshop* at his Malibu Colony beachside home. Three months into th'future I would attend one of these gatherings, but now Hank was on the phone with Zahn and the two of them were bantering, kidding each other some.

All I heard was Hank's side of this conversation; however I'll bet this is how it went:

Curtis:  "Well how's it going Hank?"

Hank:  "Pretty good, Curtis. How's your book from N.D. doing?

Curtis:  "Oh they're not doing very good getting it out there. Eh, not so hot, Hank. How's *It Catches My Heart in Its Hands* doing?"

Hank:  "All sold out! It's aahhhlll sold out, Curtis. OK! OK! See ya then, Bye Bye. . ."

Hank hung up and laughed, really happy, enjoying himself more than at any other time that evening of my first visit. He made obvious to me his satisfaction at getting th'better of Curtis Zahn. Clearly, Bukowski didn't care much for the Malibu Colony writer. I just watched, took a gulp of my beer, and watched Hank glow in happiness and some sort of debt paid

41

back in spades—squared. Zahn was what I would call upper crust L.A. Literary. He and Hank were about the same age. I guess they were peers—competitors—seeking the Brass Ring of Modern Literature. Fighting each other and a thousand others over it. Zahn would disappear. You know what would happen to Charles Bukowski.

During the phone call Hank showed me his *rascal side*. He was wonderful, an old delightful scoundrel. A master . . . a style . . . a confidence. One had better be with him because there was no beating this man, especially by someone as inexperienced as myself. I celebrated with him while silently realizing he was a tough son of a gun. That's why I was mostly reticent, keeping my yapper shut. What could he learn from me? Maybe something about what the young were up to. Maybe it heartened him a little to find out there was at least one among the young who could keep his mouth shut.

Hank had a good time. Not once during those seven hours or so did he show the least ire, sadness, disappointment with me. Through the years he would, but not that first evening.

## 10

The first 23 years of my life I didn't write nor did I read much, other than school textbooks. I cheated on a test in grammar school concerning *A Midsummer-night's Dream*. My fear of being caught by the teacher carried over into a general fear of creative literature as a whole.

At 23 I married Ruby, a UCLA English major. I was in my second year of UCLA Law School. Ruby would read Wordsworth, Shelley, Keats, maybe some Blake to me in bed prior to us making love and going to sleep. I didn't understand much of what she was reading. It almost seemed a foreign language to me, all that classic English poetry. Our marriage lasted three weeks. My brain felt like it had been split in half. I thought I had known it all, and I had not known shit.

Then a fellow law student, Stephen Malley, quoted a very short Blake ode to me. I'd been at his apartment with several other law students, part of a study group preparing for Torts or Contracts or whatever. Malley could see I was an emotional wreck. He had met Ruby a few times. He knew about our breakup. Our study session is finishing up and Malley rises, walks toward his kitchen, stops a moment, turns toward me, says, "Steve, listen to this . . . it's called 'Eternity.' 'He who binds to himself a joy, does the winged life destroy; But he who kisses the joy as it flies, lives in eternity's sun rise.'"

Well, I listened to it. It's the first poem I ever absorbed

43

in my life. It fit. I was that fuck who tried to bind Ruby to me. I most definitely was he. "Who wrote that?" I asked Malley. "William Blake," he answered. The next day I purchased *The Portable Blake*—728 pages, Viking Press, $2.25. I know because that same copy is exactly five inches to the left of my typewriter right now. My copy is 31 years old. William Blake explained to me where I'd gone wrong. Now (1963) I could understand. Being able to understand reduced my odds of self destruction about fifty percent. Suddenly poetry meant a great deal to me. And of course, like any young jackass this happens to, I began writing poems myself.

The point is that when I met Charles Bukowski less than two years later, I was a virtual blank canvas as far as my being indoctrinated into any special school of modern poetry. Nor was I a disciple of any single poet, other than Antonin Artaud. I had sat in on Jack Hirschman's UCLA Poetry Class, listened close as Hirschman read Dylan Thomas, Robert Creeley, Allen Ginsberg, Antonin Artaud, Walt Whitman, Leroi Jones, Lenore Kandel, Michael McClure, Charles Olson, William Carlos Williams, Jacques Prevert, D.H. Lawrence, Kenneth Patchen, and many more. Hirschman arranged for local poets to read before the class. I remember Alvaro Cardona Hine and Gene Frumkin. Frumkin made one comment during a question and answer session which I've never forgotten. I don't recall the question, just his answer, "Oh I wouldn't want to be presumptuous." I had been writing poems for only a few weeks when I heard this. My whole early theory about my poetry writing was that *poetry is th'place to be presumptuous!*

Poetry was no place to restrain oneself as far as I was concerned.

A few months later I mailed a copy of my first self-published book to Gene Frumkin. He wrote back telling me that there was only one poet out there whose poetry was as *raw* as my own, and that I would be well advised to contact that other raw poet. This fellow's name was Charles Bukowski. Sometime during the next year I got the chance to ask Jack Hirschman how he felt about Charles Bukowski's work. I had never heard Hirschman read a Bukowski poem in Hirschman's Poetry Class. Said Jack Hirschman: "Oh Charles Bukowski, he's the last of the alcoholic poets." He said this to me as if "The Alcoholic Poets" were a separate school of poetry, one man away from utter extinction.

In another year or so I would be placing a copy of my just completed *Earth Rose* meat poetry tabloid into the pigeon-hole box of Professor Jack Hirschman inside UCLA's English Department Main Office. I also managed to place fresh new copies inside about 30 other pigeonholes of faculty members. HO! A few weeks after this I was informed Hirschman had read from my *Earth Rose* before his Poetry Class. He read a poem titled "True Story" by Charles Bukowski. Apparently the class got a bit excited by the "FUCK HATE" headline facing them as Hirschman read from the inside page.

Right next to Bukowski's "True Story" poem was a poem by myself in which I had written a line with Jack Hirschman directly in my *INNER GUT VISION*.

"The limp professor in the academy, his balls
cut off and he knowing it, living off it!"

I think I misquote my punctuation a little, but within six more months Hirschman managed to give A's to all his students in that Poetry Class, go wacko one day in front of this class, and be fired by the UCLA Administration. I would bet all my chips that Jack Hirschman would still be teaching Poetry at UCLA today, almost 30 years later, had *Earth Rose* failed to bloom.

II

My second visit to Hank's De Longpre pad was altogether different than my first. Neeli* was there. He was hyperkinetic. He kept moving, walking here and there, couldn't seem to relax. I'd never known of nor met Neeli before. He seemed to have a great need to gain the attentions of eyes, all eyes of folks who happened to be in the same room as him. As restful and peaceful as was my first visit to Hank's place, this one was excitable and never quiet.

Neeli just couldn't sit still. He kept at his beer as did Hank and myself, but Neeli had to continue to walk back and forth to nowhere in particular, in and out of Hank's kitchen, into the bathroom, out of and back into the bathroom, from one wall to the other, bouncing around like a human-sized ping pong ball. I was getting somewhat dizzy just watching him. He's lighting a cigar, he's suddenly reading his own poetry aloud, he's up and down and spilling his beer and knocking things over and trying to find some important magazine among the hundreds on Hank's front room shelves. Hank seemed to tolerate all this pretty well. I think maybe Neeli felt somewhat insecure. Maybe he worried that I was somehow trying to "steal" Hank's attentions-time-energies away from Neeli himself. I really don't know.

Neeli would begin telling me all about one of his literary projects called *Black Cat Review*—then he'd switch to bemoaning his current girlfriend woes. Suddenly he'd explain a need to

*Neeli Cherry/Cherkovski , Bukowski Biographer. See his book *Hank.*

find *right now* some issue of some mag and he'd go to Hank's book shelves and begin digging in like a dog digging for a bone, only mags and books and broadsides would fly all over instead of pebbles and dirt clods.

After two hours of this, I took off. Shit, I had a headache.

That first night I met Neeli at Bukowski's De Longpre place (1965) I remember Neeli relating several mythic stories about Bukowski to me.

One of these was a happening at some party Bukowski and Neeli attended only a few weeks earlier. Neeli told me what happened at this party with obvious *hero worship* for Bukowski, who was listening as Neeli talked it to me. Well, they were drunk at some party and everybody at the party was drunk. Bukowski apparently insulted some fellow so much the fellow left the party, then returned with a handgun. The fellow stuck the gun into the air and shouted at Bukowski. Then the fellow pointed the gun at Bukowski. Instead of quaking with fear and pleading for his life, Bukowski walked straight up to the fellow. Bukowski pushed his own beer belly in th'muzzle of the gun. Bukowski then suggested the fellow go right ahead and shoot.

The manner Neeli told me this happening made me think at the time that it's a true story—it happened—that Bukowski is definitely Neeli's Hero/Idol/Leader?/Father Figure/etc. Why the question mark after "Leader"? I didn't consciously mean to type a question mark just now after the word "Leader;" I meant to type another "/" mark. Therefore I assume my own subconscious believes Neeli really didn't think of Bukowski as Neeli's Leader.

Neeli and Hank. Hank and Neeli. Would that Neeli Cherry/Cherkovski someday write another book about Charles Bukowski *and this time let it rip.* His *Hank,* published by Random House, is a staid academic castrated thing. Neeli spent more time with Bukowski than anyone else back in those middle sixties. He slept over at Bukowski's place for weeks at a time;

they were real drinking pals. Neeli has the closest personal experience with Charles Bukowski of any writer on Earth.

## 12

Hank and Neeli and myself were drunk one night. We'd been either at Hank's De Longpre pad or at my own cave, drinking, yammering, insulting all others except us three. Hank said, "Where are the girls? We need WOMEN! Let's go get some WOMEN! Where can we go? I need WOMEN now! What are we doing here? This is empty! Steve, where can we go for women? Girls? Hmmm?" (Now I remember we were here in my cave). I was just a few years out of UCLA and for some reason I thought of Lum's in Westwood, a college alumni beerhall plus lousy grilled food. There are always young blond billboard-like beauties at Lum's, I knew. So we drove to Lum's in Westwood. It was about 10:30 P.M., maybe 1968 or so.

Lum's was packed with huge muscled ex-UCLA football players and just as many Blond Pretty Billboard Spearmint Faced 21-22-23-year old white but very tanned ex-sorority girls. Neeli and Hank and I took seats at the one empty small table next to the open but metal-faced entrance area. I had my back to the UCLA Campus—I was facing South. Neeli and Hank sat opposite facing UCLA; Hank sat to Neeli's left and we ordered huge schooners of good, cold, golden, deep golden beer. The place was packed—th'place was *packed.*

Neeli, Hank and I, not only do not fit in but we are so different than all those Beta UCLA frat alumni ex-jock types & Kappa Gamma & Theta & Pi Phi sorority all American

Cheerleader pom pom girl sorts that I'm seriously wondering why on God's Earth I was cretin-ish enough to bring Hank and Neeli and myself here.

Waitresses pushed through holding trays high with huge beer mugs and full pitchers jiggling above'em. I looked at Hank and then I looked at various Hitler master race specimens both female & male all blue eyed & real blonds and then I looked at Hank—I kept glancing at him to see what he felt about this place & these *Christian* Revelers.

Hank didn't hide his feelings—he got that bored 'what the shit' look which told me he felt all these young ones were shallow billboard zeros and looked seriously at me—in my face he looked—and I thought I heard him say, "What th'hell we come here for?"

". . . what'd you bring us here for?"

And I was asking myself this same question—it was a mistake—but this was OK with me because the general rule about Richmond was all's well unless *he doesn't make a mistake.*

Hank kept looking back over his left shoulder at various amazing tan blond young women and then he would face me again and he'd grab his mug/schooner and take a huge Bukowski-chug-a-lug. He was getting higher, drunker, more rambunctious. All the blonds seemed to know each other and also seemed to be *happy!* Maybe they were celebrating something—a UCLA football victory earlier that night? A win over USC at the L.A. Coliseum? Maybe it was something else but those hundred-plus tanned blond UCLA handsome/pretty young ones were simply *joyous* and they all absolutely treated Hank and Neeli and myself as if we were *in toto invisible.*

Hank got drunker and started swinging his left arm out behind him at some of those ultra perfect tight girl-asses which were well within his reach. I got anxious! These fuckers were violent: these were Hitler's people and they could suddenly pick us three up and carry us, pass us from blond tanned claws to claws over their heads to Lum's Kitchen Gas Oven and *nobody would know a thing!* We could be cooked with wieners and burgers and chips and secreted out Lum's backdoor and stuffed in garbage cans and . . . but fortunately this didn't happen that night.

Hank was going even more sort of ape-crazy now swinging his left arm and graspy fingers out behind him, behind to his left, precisely ass level with the standing blond tan girls trying to squeeze through the Aryan college crowd. Then Hank would face front and face me and grab his big mug and gulp again longer and deeper. I was pissed at myself for bringing Hank and Neeli to this place. I was getting more *scared*. Hank began making palm/fingers contact with *real beautiful young tight girls asses* and ". . . oh my . . ." I thought, this is it.

I was wrong. When Hank grabbed and squeezed a girl's butt/gluteus maximus/buns each time the girl would sort of look around and down and see Hank and *then* (I tell you this is completely true) proceed to give forth a small yet moderate-toothy warmish cute smile sort of vaguely in Hank's direction. It was as if she really liked it and enjoyed such fingers/attention/touch of the authentic Apollo Sun God/master scribe magic pet-touch-caress, and what was peculiar to me was that when this girl (there were about five different girls) looked and glanced vaguely toward (level and downward glance) Hank, it was as if she didn't see him and was sort of looking through *whoever did it* and *whoever did it* was invisible to her. But this was just a wee side experience, a small warm enjoyable tangent, practically *unnoticeable* by her and within two or three seconds she looked ahead of her trying to find a crack in the standing meshed bodies so she could squeeze deeper into Lum's Beerhall. "Amazing amazing absolutely Grace" is what I thought to myself. For me it was surprise and paradox and one more miracle of Hank's unique Magic, this time while *out in th'public un*limelight.

Jesus man, I tell you I was stunned. After this same exact thing happened with blond tan cutie #3, I lost my fearful-

51

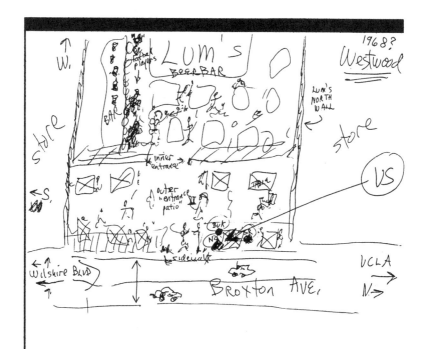

*Seating arrangement at Lum's restaurant. Drawing by Steve Richmond.*

ness. Neeli? He sat in his chair occasionally gulping his beer and kind of huffing and puffing in place and mumbling a little about what a group of shallow unappealing young folks we were in th'midst of. I think Neeli didn't react at all to Hank's moves. Neeli hung out with Hank about 50 times more than I and so Neeli probably knew full well there was nothing, nothing at all to get scared about. Hank was Magic and Neeli was Hank's door-stop. Hank wanted Neeli to be more than a door-stop but Neeli didn't seem to want to be promoted beyond his expertise.

I don't remember us leaving Lum's, nor which of us

drove, but I have a blurred trace of memory that Neeli was the only one of us to order some food. Neeli took care of business first when food was served him. I knew there was no way nor anything I could say at all to Hank to restrain his left arm grab/swings.

## 13

*Laugh Literary and Man the Humping Guns*, co-edited and published by Neeli Cherry and Charles Bukowski, will be active for three issues. Bukowski, during one of our get-togethers, is sitting in his De Longpre front room and explains to me that Neeli is really carrying the load with the magazine. Neeli is getting the mag printed, distributed, edited, taking care of checks and subscriptions and mailings, etc. Buk tells me there's just no way he could begin to do these things, take care of such duties.

When issue #1 came to life a Preface of sorts written by Neeli related how he asked me to co-edit and I stated, "No." This really didn't bother me a bit because issue #1 printed maybe a half dozen of my very best gagaku poems. I remember telling Neeli something close to, "No, I don't want to be an editor; I just want to read my own stuff. I'll read the whole mag when it comes out." During that same year or two I had published *Earth Magazine*. Everyday's mail included six to 12 packets of submitted poetry from writers all over the planet. Those packets had been piling up for several months as I'd been finally unable to continue reading through them. I felt like I'd become drowned in it all. This is why I declined Neeli's offer to co-edit *Laugh Literary*.

It's around this time a collating party is announced. *Laugh Literary #2* will be collated and stapled together at this party to take place on a weekend evening at Buk's De Longpre residence. I'm asked to give Harold Norse a ride. I do. As Norse and I enter I see about 25 people or perhaps more. Buk's front room is packed with human beings. Yes, there're Frances and Marina Bukowski. There's Alvaro Cardona Hine with a gorgeous blond. There's big John Thomas. Neeli. There're a whole bunch of people I've never seen before and I don't know. Collating is going on. Frances seems to be doing most of the actual work. Bukowski himself is drinking a beer, standing, talking to various persons I don't recognize. He seems to be staying away from the collating activities; stapling area too. Bukowski is moving around talking to folks, drinking, really just having a good time socializing.

Neeli is half working on putting issue #2 together and half talking with various folks in attendance. I stand off to one side sipping a beer and watching all this interaction. I remember an hour or so passed and then somehow all or most all these people were sitting on the front room floor facing Hank's sofa. Hank was talking to everyone, perhaps making a toast of thanks to each person, then making a grand toast for *Laugh Literary #2* itself, a wish of Good Luck to its future.

I distinctly remember Alvaro Cardona Hine, a poet I had heard read a few years earlier in Jack Hirschman's UCLA Poetry Class. A suave handsome fellow, dark olive skin, well trimmed black beard, a sophisticated appearing sexy blond in a black low cut silken cocktail dress on Alvaro's arm. Alvaro Cardona Hine had recently published an Alan Swallow-produced collection of poesy. It seemed to me Hine's work rather resembled Octavio Paz's in manner and style and imagery and . . . I don't remember any of his lines, just the Latin lover sort of semi Don Juan grace.

If Bukowski could be described as rough and sometimes raging and ragged and boil ridden and roaring emotions, Hine was the opposite—so smooth and polished and almost slick with a sheen. Alvaro Cardona Hine.

What I most remember of that "party" is Bukowski

talking with so many of the 35 or more people in his front room; Bukowski not talking much or maybe not at all with myself, as if maybe semi-avoiding me. I not talking to anyone really, just standing, drinking my beer, helping for a minute with some collating, and wondering why Bukowski and I would many times be in this same room, just us two, drinking for four or five hours.

During 1965-1966 those customers who enter my "Earth Books & Gallery" will purchase various Charles Bukowski poetry collections at a two to one ratio over all the other magazines, chapbooks, and paperbacks for sale. A good third of the folks who walk in will ask aloud for works written by Charles Bukowski.

# 14

I asked Hank for advice—once he said, "DRINK, WRITE, AND FUCK."

This came right after I complained about being bored about something. "Only the boring get bored," he commented. He was about nine feet from where I now type . . . his back to me as he was headed to my head—for a beer piss.

Another time, at his De Longpre pad, I believe, I was leaving and heard his last words to me, "Never under-estimate th'woman . . ."

He also included this phrase in a letter. I could be wrong about whether a letter or in person or . . . No! I know he said it aloud right in this room as he moved to the head because I remember his back. "Only the boring get bored."

Then me, ". . . so what should I do?"

"DRINK, WRITE, AND FUCK!"

He was convinced. Not a doubt in his tone of speaking. Strong orders. I was pleased because I knew he wouldn't order me to write if he felt in th'least I couldn't write.

# 15

Visiting and getting visited by Hank Bukowski. He comes to my poetry bookshop, "Earth Books & Gallery," about two or three times each month, always with a big brown bag. Always two sixpacks. He always walks in and sits in the only big old stuffed easy chair and he opens two cans. Always he's alone when he visits my shop and always the shop is empty when he enters and sits. Always he's quite relaxed and seems very at peace with himself. Several times I am working in the back area which is a portion of the shop about a quarter of the shop's area. A large bamboo curtain hangs from the ceiling and I use it to separate rear from front "retail" area.

Several times when I take a look into the "retail" area I see Hank already sitting down and sipping his beer and there is a second beer ready for me, on the table a few feet in front of him. Always I walk out and thank him as I take that beer for a fine swig. ("God what a great man—What a Great Fucking Man In My Shop!" is exactly what I just right now distinctly heard me whisper to me.)

Maybe he visits because I've put his *Crucifix in a Deathhand* and *Confessions of a Man Insane Enough To Live with Beasts* and *Cold Dogs in the Courtyard* and even a copy of *Flower, Fist and Bestial Wail* in the window. I mean there are only about seven books in "Earth's" front display window and Hank has four spaces and I just one with *Hitler Painted Roses* and then there're *Ole #2* and perhaps Wantling's *Down Off &*

58

*Out* from Ole Press. Anyhow, when Hank visits my shop he brings two sixpacks and says things like "Why don't you call John Bryan and pick up those 700 copies of his mag, *Notes From the Underground,* and give them away in here?"

Within three weeks copies of this mag are distributed gratis from "Earth."

Hank begins visiting my cottage about two blocks from my shop. (I don't mind the word "my." Hypocritical humility ain't for me anymore. Thank you Mr. Al Berlinski). Anyhow, when Hank visits my cottage he always, at first, brings his little Marina. He brings her along every few months and she is exactly two inches taller each time and she always sits next to him on my sofa and she always is silent and always sitting on his left and always leaning her right cheek against Hank's left shoulder. Oh how she loves her daddy. Oh how he loves his baby daughter. This is superb warmth for my eyes. Their warmth makes me feel good.

Well, after meeting Hank the first few times I relate my impulsive idea to him. "If I bring over a tape recorder you want to record something? I can just leave it until you tell me to come and get it."

He says "Yeah, Ok."

I'm about 25 years old when I get this idea and he's about 45. I'm hoping he will talk into the mike for ten or even 15 minutes because I've discovered in talking with him that he talks just like he writes. I borrow one of those large old clunker tape recorders from a friend of mine. This friend is six years younger than myself and when I mentioned why I wished to get Hank's words recorded this friend of mine, a 19 year old kid, immediately said "Hey you can use my recorder, sure, go ahead, take it—please!" I mean he pushed the tape recorder on me so I could loan it to Hank. Michael Pollak was the kid's name—Michael Pollak, 1944-1985. Archangel Mike who two decades later would gulp a whole glass of liquid angel dust. Something in Mike really wanted to help me get a recorder to

Hank. I didn't know that Mike had even heard of Charles Bukowski.

Hank would always write me and ask/tell me when to visit him; he was still at his De Longpre pad. I took that recorder to him and he had me set it on his coffee table in front of his old sofa. ("We are talking old Salvation Army leftover type of furniture both at his place and mine too," I just now said aloud. It's a damn good thing I talk aloud to myself when I write—about one full sentence every five or ten minutes. I'm sure it's my conscience.) OK, the recorder is in Hank's place and he and I only talk about it for a minute or so, he saying he will see what happens, maybe he won't feel like doing it, whatever. Then we drink beers. He always drinks about three sixpacks and I always drink between 11 and 13 beers. I can tell he feels it's important he drink more than I, and he always does. Twenty years later I will finally realize he is winning every time because he's outfoxing me. For every two beers he downs he pissed once and yes, retched too. I can hear muffled retch sounds behind his bathroom door. I mean, Hank was a *beer bolemic*. We drink for about three hours and then Hank always offers to let me sleep it off on his sofa and I always said, "No, I'm OK, I'll take it easy." I remember now there were several times I awoke the next morning without a single memory about that drive 12 miles home. Maybe it was 15 miles.

Two weeks later I return to Hank's, making the biggest mistake of my life. I take that back. It was a *giant* mistake bringing along my girlfriend, Nancy Moore K. The year must be 1966 now because Nancy and I got together in 1966. I had brought a previous girlfriend, Anna, to visit Hank about five months earlier and Hank had taken to Anna. He'd hugged her and obviously felt she was a wonderful young woman. Just as Anna and I were leaving Hank stood up and moved like a fine Grandpop to Anna who was standing too and smiling and happy and laughing a bit like a fine loving Granddaughter. Hank asked, "OK if I kiss you goodbye?" And she said, "sure," and they gave each other a wonderful happy peck farewell. Anna did the art on the cover of *Confessions of a Man Insane Enough To Live with Beasts*.

Since Anna and Nancy were both born on November 27th, I'd thought that Hank would enjoy Nancy's company as much as Anna's. It didn't work out this way. It was a few hours after the sun set when Hank opened up and let Nancy and me into his De Longpre cave. I noticed the tape recorder right where I'd set it down on the coffee table. Hank had been drinking and he seemed more anxious and more serious and sort of antsy irritated. Maybe it had been a shit day for him. Immediately I could tell Hank didn't feel anything good about Nancy. He greeted her in a perfunctory way, just sort of said 'hello' and moved his eyes off her and then moved away from us at an angle to his right rear.

He told me he had filled both sides of the tape—all 90 minutes. I was happy and surprised about this and also wondering why it was so cool between Nancy and Hank as compared to so warm months ago between Anna and Charles Bukowski. Dual fucking feelings in me! Great on th'tape! What's cookin' between those two!?

Hank tells me he wants to play right now all 90 minutes of the tape he has recorded. Actually, I didn't want to hear it then; I wanted to grab it and take it to my own lair, relax, then hear it at my leisure. Hank figured since he gave his soul, inner gut vision, all his heart, he had the right to play all 90 minutes now. He figured that I should take th'man who made the tape, as well as the tape, at least for 90 minutes. He was certainly right. It didn't bother me much; in fact I was looking forward to hearing him read on tape with him a few feet away from me! Most likely this would be the first time he would hear it too. Bukowski started the machine—his voice came alive from the machine—classic of course, and I knew it. Bukowski sat back on the sofa, lit his first cigar of th'evening. All was OK there for the first five to ten minutes. Hank began getting a little more

61

perturbed. I didn't know why. It was like a slow crescendo of irritation building in him. His body language became more staccato, but over many minutes, not suddenly. The light was very dark orange/gold . . . many shadows played on the walls. There was a dim orange glow . . . dark. When he'd rise and go to his kitchen for another beer his shadow loomed on walls.

BOOM! Something Bukowski heard on the tape must have cracked open a fissure in him and Mount Bukowski exploded. Rose to his feet and hurled his half filled beer can against the wall opposite him, right into the false fireplace facade, SPLAT. BOOM! I didn't know what had pissed him off, set him off. Maybe he felt he was giving all he had; giving all his guts, to a couple of rich kids who didn't deserve it, who had no idea what they were hearing, no idea of th'pain, dues paid in triplicate.

He exploded. It was the first time I ever saw him explode. Roaring like a King Lion who just had his tail bitten off by a Purple Baboon! Or something like that.

I had hair down to my backbone. What was he giving his soul to a goddamn hippy for? And, that billboard blond hippy bitch?

Charles Bukowski was an active volcano and Nancy and I had just witnessed an eruption. In a few minutes he calmed, sat back down, re-lit his cigar, listened to th'continuing tape play Bukowski reading poetry by Bukowski. After several more minutes he rose up and walked to his kitchen for another beer. Came back in, sat down, and the three of us listened to the rest of the tape just as if there had been no eruption at all.

I don't remember much after that— it was all pro forma: carry the machine out to the car; thank Hank; in fact all I do remember is Nancy pissed off at me when I began the drive back to Ocean Park. She half whispered half hissed, "Why did you take me along?"

She said that as if I'd taken her with me into some mens' room at a service station and forced her to give a blowjob to some wetback taking a shit.

That's how she said it. It was obvious she didn't like Bukowski. He didn't kiss her goodbye like he'd kissed Anna.

About a week later Nancy told me she dreamed about Bukowski. She told me this as if I better watch out, she just might sneak back to his pad one night or early morn and throw a pebble against his bedroom window.

What a girl. What a guy. Fuck th'world.

16

The best early days were during Hank's visits here with his daughter. He was a different man when here with Marina, who was only four or five when he first visited. Maybe all total about seven or nine visits here with her during the 1965-1969 years.

For me all those visits sort of meld into one gentle and warm time. No one of these visits stands out in my memory. It was when he came alone or with Neeli or with Linda King or with Linda and her sister, a real estate agent, that specific acts and revelries and wildnesses are in my memory.

He also would on occasion bring his girl friend at the time. He brought Frances first, then Linda King, and before Linda he brought his Brazilian gal to my Venice candleshop; he brought Liza Williams; a gal he met in Houston at his reading there; another young woman whose name escapes me; and another woman I met at the Sea Lion Restaurant in Malibu. Her Volks van broke down up there and he called me and asked for a ride.

In May of 1969 I re-rented a five-thousand-square-foot business building, a retail store building located at Venice Boardwalk and Rose Avenue. I'd rented the same building three years earlier for a place called "Earth Rose." That lasted a year. Then I went back with candlemaking in mind—a new thing I called "tree candle" which so many folks wanted to buy at first sight. Hank visited about the fifth week the store was open and he walked in the back door and with him was his Brazilian woman. They were jolly together and seemed a little beer high. It was a weird visit.

She looked somewhat a bull dyke, thick and stocky, though not a heavyweight bull D., a middleweight. I don't know her name. Hank and she came in the back door and stepped down the seven steps into my shop's rear work area; maybe seven 55 gallon oil drums full of heated liquid wax, a single gas burner beneath each, a giant steel candle wheel . . . anyhow they were happy and high and did some dancing while I watched them enjoy one another. Hank got behind her and held her and humped her butt and she liked it and laughed and laughed and he laughed and played like an old satyr who has grabbed a girl and has just what he wants today. They liked each other and they rather ignored me as I leaned against a work table and quietly watched them do their show-fun-thing. I wondered a little why they came, just driving around to this place and that place and an hour later the place over there. I was one of the stops. They had a little hug and dance and laugh together and hug and dry hump while standing and it was OK with me.

She had a short bull dyke haircut—sort of sloe-eyed sensuality on olive skin—and I could tell she knew Hank and knew his work. She knew, maybe more than I, just how fine Hank was in his writing. She was the first woman I'd seen Hank with after Frances, Marina's Ma. Maybe Hank wanted me to see that he was now moving on. Maybe he wanted to make sure I didn't wonder if he was bi or gay. Maybe he was walking down to the beach, down Rose Avenue and saw the back door open and he was with her and he came in on impulse. He had talked about her a few times before and written a little in some letters, and now I see her olive face and it's better looking, even resembling Sophia Loren's face some. It's an olive skin Sophia face with that depth of sensual sex-thing that even is more erotic because of a hint of bisexuality.

Ah well, I never saw her again and Hank never mentioned her to me again. Hank's women were almost all full bodied just like those females he would draw with large breasts, and legs from top of thigh showing, and all in high heel shoes.

No skinny gals for Hank, none that I saw anyway.

He liked to talk about women—a little literary talk but 85% of our conversations he'd bring back to women—what/why/who/when/why/why.

That was it, the Brazilian woman. Down the back stairs and dance around a bit and joke and kind of a put-on leer as he hugged her from behind and humped her big ass and she laughed and humped her ass backwards and they made a pretty good couple, on my eye. I really can't remember them leaving and the last I see of myself I haven't moved an inch, still standing/leaning against a four foot high work table, watching.

Feels a bit like I'm in a movie theater watching a series of shorts and/or vignettes and now this one's over and lights come up and I'm sitting there wondering yes or no re buttered popcorn.

17

Hank often came over when I was off somewhere. He'd leave little notes of varying sorts. He was always welcome except once. He was pounding on the door and he was with Neeli. They were boisterous out there and kept pounding. It was a very sunny day and I think early afternoon. *"HEY OPEN UP PRECIOUS! WHERE TH'HELL ARE YOU?"*

I was in here and didn't want to see anybody; I can't remember why. I do remember I didn't want anyone in here and so I didn't open up. This pissed them off. Beer-drunk angry, they started yelling insults and they walked back toward Hollister Avenue and kept ranting various profane crap.

I could see them. I peeked out a front window and I noticed how truly agitated both of them had become. Both threw their beer cans out on my front kikuyu weed grass. When I saw them do that I knew I was right about not letting them in. I had a brief impulse to go out there and kick their asses but I quickly restrained myself out of one part laziness, one part energy retention, and one part knowledge that they didn't know for sure I was in here. Possibly I had yelled out from in here, and they did know I was here. I can't remember this particular.

What they did and how they acted that day, as I saw them through the window, made me figure they were simply two more assholes on a planet of billions of th'same.

(I just said aloud, in an offhand semi-sarcastic voice, "Neeli was a little prick.")

He wanted to be Bukowski so bad that when I'd be talking with him in some short conversation, gossip, and for the first time in this conversation bring up the word "Bukowski" he would suddenly *for the first time* have a facial tic. A huge tic. I found it interesting and obviously revealing. I decided his tic was from his wish to *be Bukowski*. And so in Neeli's biography, *Hank,* it seems Neeli so often *gets in front of Bukowski.* Why would a man start a facial tic when only one word is spoken in his presence?

The day they were here together pounding at my door and I wouldn't let them in and they got pissed and ranted outside and angrily threw their beer cans on my front yard—my unmowed weeds. Well, I use a weed whacker now and it resembles a lawn—I water it because my water is ripped off from poor Owens River Valley. They left right after tossing their cans. Buk was driving his little Volks; maybe it was still the Dodge Dart; but they left and I was glad they were gone. Bad drunks. Two bad drunks. I knew one of them was a great great writer but I didn't give a shit. It was around 1970-71. Maybe not. Maybe it was 1969 or 1973. Why do I recall it? It is sewn to something in my brain. I often remember this "incident" as I do about one or two hundred others. That's why I'm writing this, all th'warts and th'ups and downs and arounds, too.

Today is July 2, 1994. Buk is gone so he can't fight back. Or is he gone? I didn't love him that day. I guess this is my main point. He was just another schmuck in a sea of them. That day was a rare one, though. Nine out of ten times I was with Buk he and I were Pals and the sea of assholes was everyone else.

Well, damn it. Was just making a copy of this page in my back room and remembered one other time I didn't let Hank in. He wanted to take a shit. His two previous visits he'd knocked and when I opened up his very first words were, "Can I take a shit?"

Yes. Yes. Try Chevron up the block.

There was no Chevron up the block. (I'm talking to myself again, "What the fuck was he doing?")

It's obvious.

It's OK. I liked such supposed little battles with Hank. It sublimated our natural human male bull competitive urges to cut one another's throats, instead.

**18**

One day in 1967 or 1968—it is a day during the period Hank drives his beloved Volks Bug—he loves this car as no other—he telephones me from a pay phone on the Santa Monica Mall. He tells me, "Steve, my car is over at 'Bug Builders'. I started walking and I'm lost. I don't know where I am but it's killing me. I'm trapped. Steve, can you save my ass? I'm getting murdered here. They're surrounding me."

That's the gist of what he told me, asked me. It's been about twenty-seven years since this call and I have to be misquoting some. He's able to describe his location well enough that I soon know exactly were he is, where he feels stranded and paranoid. He's on the Santa Monica Mall, the old Third Street section between Broadway and Wilshire—Third Street has been closed off and changed into a 70 or 80 foot wide shoppers' walk. The city's idea to help business has instead ruined business along this four block long shopping zone. Higher class shops have vacated and left only vacancies and bargain basement type stores. The folks who now walk along this Mall seem Zombified, had their bodies snatched, souls replaced with something alien and mechanized, gone. The folks are just GONE who move along this Mall. Bukowski is caught in the middle of them. He's petrified. He feels a vacuum suck working on him, also.

He telephones me to rescue him. It's around 11 A.M., a weekday, sunny—way too bright and sunny, rather hot, and I tell him I'll drive over and get him *RIGHT NOW*. He is to be standing at Third Street and Santa Monica Boulevard. I'm on my way.

I drive over and spot him right away. He's standing in shadows a few feet from a stark beige wall—The Hollywood Citizens Bank—and he sees me and immediately begins moving quick toward my car. He is obviously shaken, his body hunched, shoulders hunched in pinching his chest some. He is hustling the hell quick to my car to get away from The Santa Monica Shoppers' Mall. God Bless him.

I right now see Hank walking toward my car, me in it stifling with magnified *heat of sun* pouring in through front windshield on me. I'm sweating lots, *HOT AS SHIT*, and Buk is walking. Why is it taking him so damn long to get to my passenger side car door and get in? He's still in shadows somehow, shadow of that 50 to 100 foot straight high stark beige wall of Citizens Bank Building, my car facing toward Pacific Ocean three blocks west of me, Pacific glittering way too much ocean.

I look to my right through passenger side window. I'm driving a fire engine red two-door Chevy II wagon. He (Bukowski) is walking Fast-Fast. I can tell obviously he is hustling to my car but he doesn't seem to get much closer at all. How can he walk so hurriedly and yet not cover the 100 feet or so between himself and my passenger door? I'm fucking stifling forgive me Wilma McDaniel stifling in my driver's seat with sun rays all over my front neck & chest and damn it is perspiring like wet mad hot.

I look to my right and Buk is hurrying hurrying to my car—me—he is still in cooler shadows—grey and *gray and grey too*—shadows.

("Ehh/Ahhh why does it always have to be such great Magic when he's around?" I just muttered/whispered to myself.)

Emotions, Thoughts, Alertness, "on my toes feelings," all intensified and sort of *HYPER-ENED* when I'm with Bukowski. The first reason that comes to me is: I suppose/guess

I want to make a good impression, not get slovenly or careless with my manners, ideas, spoken words, facial expressions, etc. Self-conscious?

("I suppose so," I say slowly to myself.)

But all my whining above is just so much less than my unforgettable vision of Hank walking quickly to my car to escape that Mall. Most of all there is anxiety in his front body language. He is experiencing about 45% to 65% anxiety as he hustles to my Chevy II. He gets in. I drive to Ocean Avenue, turn left, head south to my shack. Maybe we had a few beers? I can't remember. I do vaguely remember dropping him off several hours later at "Bug Builders" on 5th Street in Santa Monica.

("The sun is just too damn bright right now," I just said, noting how the sun was exactly th'same on that day almost 30 years ago.)

Hmm, I like it overcast and cool.

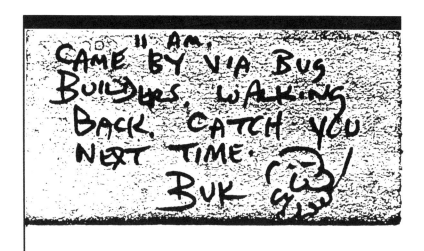

*Note left by Bukowski at Steve Richmond's door.*

**19**

Hank and I were walking north on Venice Boardwalk. Hank was on the ocean side to my left. We had been at the apartment—third floor beachfront—of a woman with a pretty face, and Hank said to me somewhere along the walk, "pretty like a billboard face."

We'd been at her apartment for almost three hours. We got there around one and left around four in the sunny afternoon. It was sun coming in her windows the full time we were partying. A few other *humans* were *partying* too.

Hank knew her and took me along. He wasn't that anxious to go to her place but it seemed as if it was the least dull of his choices. I was with him as a foil perhaps, from his side. From my side I was just with him as an almost in toto obscure 10-year-younger sidekick to a very famous great scribe. It was in th'70's about 20 years ago and I am now convinced he's still the greatest. Well, I was walking with him and he was wearing slacks and a sportscoat and short sleeve white or pastel dress shirt and no tie. I don't remember what I wore. I remember the walk as if he's just to my left right now. He sort of pulls his chin in, or it seems so to me, as he walks at my left. His expression and his upper front body language is a moderate amount of dis-something. I'm trying to figure: not disconcerted, not disheartened. He's a little *irritated* actually; it didn't quite go as he wished it had gone at the apartment, I guess.

Her boyfriend kept coming in and going out. He was a

blond fellow about four feet ten inches and Hank would walk up to this fellow as this man would walk in the front door of Joanna's apartment and Hank would stand right in front of this fellow and look down at him. Hank must have been a good foot taller and he would bend his face down. Hank would stand tall as he could and just angle his own face down to the blond man's face, which would turn up and . . . no hostility at all. Pure amicable interaction that day between Hank and the woman and myself and the blond boyfriend, almost a crew-cut blond man about 27.

The floor was without rugs, one of those well cared for natural wood floors. Against the south wall she'd put a double mattress on the floor and strewn-thrown-placed many colorful pillows and covered the mattress with Indian bedspread (Madras?). Hank would lie on the mattress with his head against the pillows.

Hank drank, and talked like he writes. It was the first time I listened to his words closely, and he was making sure his words were like his unique poesy. Amazing words he was saying, one of a kind images. Charles Bukowski, if he wished to, talked just like he wrote, and anyone hearing him had to marvel as I did then. I remember specifically thinking for a moment, "JESUS CHRIST . . . well, yes—Jesus Christ he is, talking those Bukowski words no one else can write nor talk nor even anything . . ."

I mean it was great Bukowski poetry he was talking. Not fancy, not with any degree of trying. It was natural and amazing poetry and images and . . . ("I couldn't believe what th'fuck I was hearing," is how I right this second said it aloud to myself.)

The boyfriend and Hank made it two men there interested in Ms. Bull. She smiled a lot and played her drums and moved around her living room. Her apartment was the front view third floor (top floor) pad but she kept curtains over the view windows so I never did see out of them that day. Daylight, lots of it, came in through open side wall windows, the southside wall. We were socializing and drinking beers though maybe there was white wine too, and Hank while lying down—rather resting his back against pillows—suddenly popped a pair of tiny white pills. He didn't attempt to hide this, just took them out and tossed them in his mouth—like Bingo. He knew I was watching him. Maybe I was bothering him a little by not going out on my own in that apartment and doing something—playing the piano, beating the drum set, anything. I wasn't doing much of anything save lying near the end of the mattress and watching them all for later vulture-ish content. (Like right now.)

It disturbed him a bit, I think. He didn't say so, but, he would sort of take on a *COME ON ASSHOLE—DO SOMETHING!* look.

We'd been drinking Miller beers, maybe up to seven sixpacks. She had her big living room set up with a set of well cared-for trap drums, a piano (a nice old good looking upright), a guitar leaning against wall, and a variety of other instruments.

Only her piano attracts Bukowski to itself. Why? Perhaps because it's most related to his typewriter. Keys on th'piano/typewriter too. He certainly works both instruments almost identically. As I watch him play the piano, it's obvious he's enjoying himself. He loves playing instruments with keys.

He sat on the piano bench and, just like he typed, kept his hands up around his upper chest, like a boxer keeping his guard up, then punched strong confident solid jabs—straight punches—to the piano keyboard. Quick, superb hand speed-punching down 45 degrees, striking the keyboard.

Somehow he makes original music. Not noise at all. Flourish, large movements, not a drop of self-consciousness, not a pinpoint of any self-repression, big motions of his body-back-neck and head, arms and hands and punching fingers, his music a part of Ives, Stravinsky, Monk, Ornette Coleman, Scott Joplin too. His music is somehow a melodious combination of all of 'em. Bukowski is a natural. It's like he's always perfectly oiled and lubed as far as making living art. Grace in motion. A man with in toto confidence regarding his creativity moves with fluid grace.

It doesn't matter if he possesses a beer belly. In fact it makes it better on my eye. If this all sounds sexual somehow th'reader is misunderstanding me. Art, the word *"ART,"* is so over used—I mean my candlemaking was not art—but until a better word comes along (human creates) Bukowski is the numero uno example of explicit body language of *THE BEST AT IT: ART*, that I've ever encountered in a man, or woman.

Including Baryshnikov.

I talk to myself now, *"I think he has me along with him because he knows someday I'm going to be writing about him. Not only someday but some many many many days."* And he wants the truth written about him, for better or worse he wants the most truthful beans possible spilled in th'future about Charles Henry Bukowski. He has read my early poetry, even written a Foreword to one of my earliest collections. He believes I'm the guy who just might be able to someday "paint th'most accurate portrait" of th'man himself, Henry Charles Bukowski.

He knows I don't give a damn whether Henry or Charles comes first on his official birth certificate. He knows I do care about him. He knows I love and revere him in my pronounced non-homo way. He knows my own Ma was correct when she told me, "you have a way with words." He knows I believe him Earth's finest scribe. He knows he's my president of America.

76

# 20

It was a bookshop about 100 feet north of Hollywood Boulevard and four or five blocks east of Western Avenue: Hank's very first poetry reading—a public reading with an admission charge and circulars mailed out weeks earlier to inform those southern Californians who had read Bukowski that they could now see him and hear him read his poetry.

I was working my candleshop at Rose and Venice Boardwalk and I received a circular in my mail. Hank had handmade the circular in multicolor ink pens and it was a vibrant rainbowy full of sun-life 8 1/2" by 11" wonderful piece of typing paper. If I had it now, I'm certain it would cost a collector hundreds to get it from me, and many many collectors would vie for it. I don't remember the name of the bookshop; I could walk 15 feet to my shelves and find it in Neeli's *Hank;* it's not important, the name of the shop.

Kenmore Avenue?—perhaps the name of the street. I went, drove and parked and it was night, around 8:30 P.M. and I guess 1970 because this is my candleshop year. I drove and parked and walked to the shop's door and there was a rather small retail room with new books neatly displayed like any good little well-stocked bookshop. But the folks in this area weren't looking at any books. They looked like fine regular young creative people, a few oldsters, there was Wanda Coleman, young and beautiful skinned and sexy.

("It's the only time I've ever seen Wanda Coleman,"

said I, just now to me. Big brass flashing hoop Afro ear-rings. "Right now I see her again. Shit, it's great to see her.")

She and I didn't speak. She didn't notice me, or if she did she decided not to look at me. I looked at her. Nice limbs, good shape, voluptuous, "ripe like a plum."

(That's what my voice said now, again, Midnight or one A.M. now 7-12-94. Maybe it's the 14th . . . who cares?) Wanda was 24 years younger the night I saw her in the shop retail area. This area was low lit and there was a pleasant gold/orange kind of shaded glow to her *gorgeous* shining just right skin. Her breasts stuck out but not too much. Sweater, I believe. "Chocolate, lovely Hershey-bar skin." Hell, I wanted to pick her up and take her back here to this cave and dine on her goddammit.

But she didn't look at me. There was a good crowd of us in the retail area. This area was a lobby that night and Hank was to read in a much larger room one entered through the door. I mean one entered the shop and about 12 feet further on was another door and then a large high ceilinged room, maybe 50 feet by 30 feet. Chairs set up in rows around a big easy chair raised up on a foot high wood platform. This "throne" chair set in the middle of this big room and about 100 or so folding chairs set around in a circle.

Packed house. It's Hank's first public reading—that's what I believed. I think it really was, "and it was a fine reading." I was the first to leave, before Hank finished reading. I got bored. I tell you the truth. Hank once told me, right here in this cave/room I type in right now, "only the boring get bored." I'd told him I was bored, I think I meant in general and he immediately said, "only the boring get bored." It was early afternoon, sunny out there, he was sort of walking to my pisser to take a beer leak. I think he said that before. I mean Hank said that so quick and prepared for it, I think it was his standard come-back when anyone said, "Oh God . . . I'm bored."

You know what I mean?

(Well, I just read the above and I got off the reading.)

I sat and saw and heard him read in nice lowered soft lights . . . and I stayed for an hour and he had everyone there with him, but not me. I mean I liked it, I liked Hank reading for the first 35 minutes. Then I got itchy. I was the only one. Maybe 100 to 120 other folks more sensitive than I, perhaps. Hank looked great in that very soft light, on his easy chair throne, reading, I remember, from *Kaa Kaa and Other Immolations*—that was one of them. I guess I was unable to feel it as well as all the others.

I like poetry on paper. Poems on Paper Away From the Sexy Crowd. It's a show.

"It's meaningless."

After an hour I slipped out and no one saw. They were with Hank. Not one peep out of this audience, he was so grand and warm grand-dad-giving, Lion-white-bearded, glowing himself, not too much, nothing showy. He was perfect. He was there. He loved this night and I needed fresh haven time. I needed to separate myself from Hank and his believers who might sit and hear him glow on with his absolutely great gift of giving, reading on, they would still be there now, never rising from their chairs for a whole almost, yes, 24 years.

Many will think—maybe I will think—I was envious, jealous, and I wanted up on the easy old cushioned chair.

I don't think so. Well, suddenly my next thought was Hank made good money that night. I would enjoy it all, for that good money would have somehow made it right. Not selling oneself for damn near nothing.

"Old men love money," wrote Confucius. "Yes, I was jealous," say I again. It was the decent pay Hank received—five bucks to get in to this reading. I don't think I paid. I was special. I was a cheap asshole.

Bah, it was an immortal reading—and everyone there *save myself* was immortal. I was mortal. Robert Peters has written of this Bukowski reading. Peters was one of the audience.

Everyone there loved it but me.

What, I ask you, is the fuck, the holy fuck, wrong with me?

"Nothing," is what I think to myself. Not a damn thing. It was Hank and the crowd—they were all as one. I was the unglue that didn't hold them together so I got up and walked/slipped out. I remember hitting the street, so quiet, no cars, a cool clear east Hollywood night, a Tuesday night, and I could finally B R E A T H E.

**21**

Bukowski? I rasp to myself, ". . . he could write about himself and make it work."

(I know. I don't know if I can get there. How's that for an awkward line? I'm in a shit mood again. Pouring sweat all day, dripping toxins out of me, cake, lemon meringue, got th'runs, must have been th'matza ball soup last night.)

Let's take it from about a year from myself bringing Ben Pleasants to Bukowski's De Longpre flat. Pleasants has written some articles for the *L.A. Free Press.* He requests that I appear at what he calls " A Bukowski Symposium." Participants will be Bukowski, Pleasants, myself, Gerald Locklin, and Ron Koertge.

Pleasants will act as moderator. We will meet around two in the afternoon at the *L.A. Free Press* main offices about three blocks east of Hollywood and Vine.

I am very proud/honored/delighted to be asked to participate. In 1975 the *L.A. Free Press* is still Southern California's premier "counter-culture" newspaper. I revel in appearing in such publications. I revel in appearing in almost all publications. The astrology pulp paperbacks suggest Bukowski is a man who by birth seeks immense fame and power *and does not hide his ambition.* These same books claim I by birth seek exactly the same but I try to keep it a big secret.

Well, it's another very sunny day in Hollywood, and I locate the "Freep" offices, a building right over one edge, the west edge, of the Hollywood Freeway. It's on Hollywood Boulevard. It's my first visit there. I walk in a small entering cubicle. A hip receptionist leads me through three or four doors in what is a maze of short hallways. The "Freep" probably gets bomb threats every two or three days. Then up some stairs and into a larger conference room. I'm last to arrive. Shit, I'm not late either.

The room is exactly how one would picture an "underground newspaper" conference room. The five men sitting at the table include the five of us I named and also Michael C. Ford. He will "sit-in" on the recorded discussions but he won't say a word.

Why? I don't know.

Maybe he's the secret government agent who financed the whole thing. Probably not. Bukowski is seated at the head of the long rectangular table, really two big square tables have been moved next to each other.

The other five men all have rather short hair and facial hair too. I'm clean shaven, my hair is a few inches above my tail bone, and I sort of resemble one of Geronimo's men. Bukowski is wearing Sears work clothes—long sleeve very dark green Sears work shirt, same material/colored pants. I would call it navy green as navy blue is too blue. Way darker than olive drab. He appears very serious, rather impatient to get this thing going. He is 55 years old. All us other five are around 35.

Everyone is serious in that fucking room. If it's 1975, and it is, the Vietnam war is over and gone. What this is, is a meeting of the Bukowski Inner Circle—The Bukowski Gang . . . ("We are a tough looking bunch of fuckers," is how I put it aloud right now) . . . because I'm peering down at a photo of us that ran in the 1975 issue of "Freep." We look very serious. Bukowski is in the middle with his right hand resting on Ben's left shoulder. To Ben's right is Koertge. I am next to Bukowski on his immediate left, shoulder to shoulder. Locklin is on my left shoulder. Behind us is a brick wall, th'sort of wall subversives might be lined up against and blasted by a firing squad.

You brought short stories and novels to poetry. A lot of your stuff is really stories.

**Bukowski:** It's just a line. I could write a poem as a short novel. That's all.

**Locklin:** I always thought that was true. In the universities, they tend to talk about restoring narrative to poetry, and that sort of thing, and as far as I'm concerned, Bukowski did it without even thinking about it.

**Richmond:** It's easier to get a poem published than it is a novel.

**Bukowski:** It's easier to get a poem rejected than it is a novel.

**Koertge:** No, it's not. It just takes longer for a novel.

**Bukowski:** No, you see, you write a novel and how many pages have you blown to the winds? A poem comes back, and you either send it out again, tear it up. Then you sit down, put on a new typewriter ribbon, and you get another poem. It's less time consumed.

**Pleasants:** There's another thing, though. A really good poem is like a stick of dynamite: it just goes off with tremendous force. Whereas a novel is another type of thing. I think in terms of power you can say it better in a poem than you can in a novel.

**Bukowski:** Yeah, if it works. . . . You mentioned John Crow Ransom. One of the only good poems he wrote was about the Catholic girls, you know. He was watching them walk by, and he said, "I know a woman" — these aren't the exact lines, but "I know a woman who is now old and so forth and so forth who was once more beautiful than any of you." And that was a powerful . . a poem can do that. . . I know what you're saying.

**Pleasants:** I wanted to ask you about the influences that made you think first of all and the in-

**Bukowski:** I didn't know what other writers had done. I just had to take those extra couple of hours, get the beer out, and to balance what was happening to me.

**Richmond:** It's got a lot to do with making your own answers to survive. You know, you read a book and there's no answer there. There's nothing worth surviving for in what you read. Nothing worth surviving for in what you see in the streets. So you go to the typewriter and you create something, and it becomes the only thing worth surviving for.

**Bukowski:** Exactly it.

**Pleasants:** What do you have to say about that, Ron?

**Koertge:** I don't think anything. I mean, not that's coherent.

**Pleasants:** In what Bukowski's done, is poetry prose? What is the distinction? What makes a poem poetry?

**Bukowski:** I don't concern myself with what's a poem, what's a novel. I just write it down — it either works or it doesn't work. I'm not concerned with "this is a poem, this is a novel, this is a shoe, this is a glove." I write it down and that's it. That's the way I feel about it.

**Pleasants:** Do you feel that way, Ron?

**Koertge:** I like having published enough so that I can send things out, and if people say we don't like this 'cause it isn't a real poem, I can just send it out again, and somebody'll say we're gonna publish this and call it prose poems or something. I don't care what they call it. But I like being in the position where I don't have to worry about it.

**Pleasants:** This is a question to Bukowski. Jeffers was a nihilist, classic definition. Are you a nihilist? And what about the influence of philosophy?

**Bukowski:** You want to find out if I know what the word nihilist means?

*Meeting of the "Bukowski Symposium" at the L.A. Free Press.*
*(L.to R.) Koertge, Pleasants, Bukowski, Richmond, Locklin.*

83

**22**

We have been mailed a finely printed extra large very heavy weight white cardboard material invitation. It's about ten inches by eight inches. Taylor Hackford has made a movie for Public Television. It is about Charles Bukowski and we have been invited to the premier celebration/showing of this 90 minute film about Charles Bukowski. It is to take place at Barnsdall Park auditorium, located at the intersection of Vermont Avenue and Hollywood Boulevard. We will take our lovely invitation with us because otherwise we won't gain entry. The modern theater facility there at Barnsdall will be filled to absolute capacity. Some guests will not find a seat. These folks will sit on the nice carpets along two glorious aisles. We will arrive early because our asses are aging and we best sit in those well-cushioned new seats.

*We are going to the movies. We are arrogant self-indulgent fools who are believed degenerate animals by some literary folks who may truly have become exactly what they have sought to become: elite.*

Oh, to be one of th'elite . . . oh, how I have worked my member nightly to be someday accepted by this select higher than all esteemed clique. One knows th'elite by how they respond to one's letters: back one postcard with one sentence. This sentence is unfailingly a line like: "Snowed under here, suggest you keep a stiff upper lip." Or perhaps, "Do what you do and let the chips fall where they may." Or maybe, "You should remember a stitch in time saves nine."

Well, it's movie night! We are very honored to be invited by special mail. We could not drip with cynicism and sour wit had we not been invited by special post. We have tucked the fine invitation into our scrapbook because we know a Charles Bukowski collector will pay dearly for this document. We are not fools. We are not even degenerates because we keep writing and our works are sometimes authentically published— even listed in Bowker's huge *Books In Print* hardbound tomes found in every bookstore worth a dime. We enjoy this especially on blues days when we have lost our identity and feel ourselves worthless human dregs of flop-dom. Failures. Unbeloved failures considered toxic tar babies by our un-fellow human beings!

We are going to the movies. Come. It's night now. It's the right date. We will have to sit on the aisle carpet if we don't leave NOW.

Envious? You bet. Only an idiot wouldn't desire a movie about his/her Supreme Creative standing among all earthlings. But I deny that I'm wracked with envy, jealousy, such lousy feelings, because what does life teach us more than envy/coveting/ill-will/begrudging/jealousy will *lead to stress—which leads directly to a melanoma,* say just behind my own right ear? So, I'm not jealous. I'm instead full of commendable hypocritical humility for Hank, happy of radiant bright crowd there wishing Hank a grand film during next two hours. Hank has my full allegiance, wish to maximum success on the spiritual/material/emotional planes of our human existence. May he always *do what he does and let his chips fall where they may.* I am for Hank, otherwise I wouldn't have driven into a city of abominable visual appearance, even at night. I am not to display honest arrogance this evening. It would be unseemly in a crowd so replete with Hollywood notables, th'hip south California counter-culture (actors like Stockwell are here, film people everywhere, lovely young

85

blonds direct from billboard modeling gigs.)

I arrive, park, enter, now about two-thirds of the audience are seated. I take a seat on the left aisle. I'm the first guest on the center section seat, left aisle, roughly two-thirds of rows from screen. There is an empty seat which remains empty for quite a long time, just to my right.

Now someone has asked me to uncross my legs, rise and allow him to cross in front of me so he can sit next to me on my right. I take a brief glance at this man. He has a few white hairs jutting out and down from his white dry chin skin, and he has long long white gray top hair. He is . . . *Frances, mother of Buk's only child.* Why does she wish to sit next to me? There are still dozens of empty seats scattered about and all are obvious to a person taking a seat. The lights are still on, bright as too sunny days in south California. Why does Frances sit directly next to me?

Is she attempting to make Hank jealous? Not a chance in hell of this. Maybe she feels I'm an OK human to have at her immediate left, during what will be an emotional experience of some heaviness for her. Linda King has been Buk's Queen for several years. Frances has been cast aside with a small monthly stipend to help support Marina, who lives with Frances, her very own mother.

I watched this film—felt/thought it a great film—it was around 90 minutes long—about one year later Public TV station KCET in Los Angeles would show a 30 minute version—and why such an abbreviated version of a great film about our own planet's finest scribe . . . why did they cut it to 30 minutes?

Obvious.

They are th'most terrible sorts of simple assholes.

After the film, a reception was announced upstairs in the gallery area. Red and white wines were to be served, along with crackers and cheese and whatnots, I believe it was also announced.

I walked upstairs.

86

The full house crowd, about 700 folks, either left or walked upstairs to the huge gallery hall. Giant paintings were up on the walls but I don't remember any of these artworks.

A long table had paper cups full of white wine and red wine. I don't recall whether or not crackers . . . hors d'oeuvres of any kind were actually available. I do remember myself moving to a spot in one corner of the giant art gallery hall, the southeast corner it was, where I stood and leaned against some kind of strongly constructed glass case which displayed something or other inside.

I drank my white wine from the paper cup and watched. For about five minutes I was relaxed and alone and at peace standing/leaning in that corner watching various humans walk around and mix a bit, schmooze really with one another, and then Neeli Cherry (later Cherkovski) walked up to me and stood next to me and chatted a bit. He seemed to be doing what I was doing—watching too.

I remember feeling not all that good about Neeli walking over to my special corner of *relative solitude* where I was *alone and relaxed and probably in a kind of one-third consciously posing for th'gals and two-thirds watching/recording/rather filming like a camera named Steve Richmond.* Neeli didn't bother me much, either. I chatted a little back at and with him. He did not walk to my "position" to bug me. He was quiet and seemed to be kind of "recording" also. I like to move to certain corners; no one can sneak up behind.

I remember seeing what seemed about one-third the number of people that had filled the auditorium downstairs. Apparently two-thirds of the audience had decided to leave rather than socialize at this reception—that is socialize OR stand in a corner and watch and record as I was, and as Neeli also was doing next to me. For awhile it seemed as if those who were at this reception were far away from me, maybe always at least 30 feet away and more. No one except Neeli seemed to move to within 30 feet of where I stood/leaned against the display case.

87

Then I saw Charles Bukowski—Hank . . . Bukowski . . . Hank . . . and John Martin either standing near one another or walking very slowly next to each other, at about a distance of 50 feet. They were chatting with a few folks. Then Bukowski and Martin moved on and chatted awhile with some other folks. Bukowski and Martin were moving slowly around/across the huge room greeting, exchanging "pleasantries," with the one-third of the film audience that chose to attend this reception.

It seemed to me, as I watched Buk and Martin, that Martin was at times introducing Bukowski to various friends of Martin. I remember feeling at one point it seemed as if Bukowski was standing in a strange kind of hunched stance, like almost a bit of a primitive husky Neanderthal type of humanoid, while Martin was upright and thinner, *and that perhaps Martin was, in a way, showing off his/Martin's prize steed.* I then thought a little about how Martin sometimes referred to the scribes he published through Black Sparrow Press as "my list," and I somehow got a notion that Martin felt his writers were his *racehorses.* Charles Bukowski was perhaps Martin's "Secretariat." These few thoughts and feelings were passing through me as I watched Martin and Bukowski relate to reception attendees. For about five minutes I watched Martin and Buk move slowly and talk to people. Again, several times Martin seemed to be introducing Bukowski to friends of Martin who had been invited, like myself, by special finely printed mailed invitations, to see this new film. *Then Martin and Bukowski began moving my way*, my way and Neeli's way as it happened. I thought to myself: *Goddamn Neeli! I should be standing/leaning here in this peaceful strategic corner* alone!

**23**

We put our soul on paper. When it's rejected, when we get back small printed rejections slips, we know our soul has been judged as shit.

And maybe it is, maybe what we submitted out there was crap. There's a Bukowski letter included in *Screams From the Balcony* which is to me. July 25, 1968 Hank is writing me that he has accepted three of my odes for the poetry magazine he's co-editing with Neeli. Do you know how that makes me feel? Not only 23 years ago when he sent it but today? Every day until I die? I've read 10,000 copies of *Screams* were sold on the first day it was available at bookstores. Ten thousand folks know Hank accepted my soul . . . three times over . . . for the only magazine he ever edited and published, *Unsuicidal*. This is how I feel. (Something in me says ". . .patience . . .")

**24**

I've been asked to give Harold Norse a ride. I'm to drive about one mile south along this seashore and pick him up and drive him to East Hollywood. Norse lives in an apartment on Paloma Walk in Venice, about 50 feet from the Venice Boardwalk.

I think he called me and asked for a ride. I'd met Norse a short time earlier when Neeli and Hank came to my Venice candleshop; got me to accompany them to visit Norse's place about three blocks south along the Boardwalk. My shop was at Rose Avenue and the Boardwalk.

Anyhow, during that first visit I was sitting in one of Norse's easy chairs reading from one of his newly published books. He walked up behind me and stood kind of leaning over my shoulder, ostensibly to see how I was taking in his writing, but actually to lurk too close to me with those shit vibes. Now I've been asked to pick up this excellent poet and drive him to Hank's place so that we might help collate *Laugh Literary #2*. OK, I'll do it. After all I'm driving a 1969 Chevy van which fortunately has its motor up high, serving as a barrier between the passenger's seat and my driver's seat.

Also, I've read and respected the works of Lorca, Rimbaud, Baudelaire, Ginsberg, as well as Burroughs' *Junky* novel, plus Norse's poetry. All these fellows are gay, or were gay—so? So I will give Norse a lift to Hank's place. I only remember that I knocked at Norse's door, he came out, we walked to my van, the sun is setting but it's still pretty light, we exchange a few courteous words, night-time comes during the drive into East Hollywood, he and I are in toto silent the whole way to Hank's.

As a boy I grew up in West Hollywood. The Oriental Theater was a block south of our family home. I'd walk down and see films about every other weekend. Gay men would be in there furtively glancing around, checking it out. Once a guy took a seat next to me and offered me popcorn. No thanks. He put his left hand on my right leg. He was twice as big as I was. I got up and took another seat.

When after-school playground football/baseball/basket-ball was over at Bancroft Junior High School, I'd hitchhike from Santa Monica Boulevard and Highland Avenue up Highland to Sunset Boulevard, then west on Sunset to Gardner Street and walk north a block home. Gays gave me rides about half the time.

"Do you ever shit around?"

"Wanna go up to the hills?"

These kinds of questions were put to me. No thanks. Several times I had to jump out of cars. Now I'm 53 and I'm convinced they're all predators and pederasts, given the chance.

Norse and I knocked at Hank's door. Someone opened up and we walked in. Somebody else gave Norse a ride home that night.

**25**

I was thinking about Harold Norse, how he was so anonymous when he lived for about one year just 50 feet off the Venice Boardwalk.

Among the tens of thousands strolling, beaching, watching the crowds walk up and down that beachside walk—Harold Norse would not be noticed at all unless one knew him. Never a bright colored piece of clothing, always navy blues and darker browns, never a loud voice, always quiet and unassuming, one of Earth's truly great poets—he easily had to be the finest scribe living in and around Venice during 1969-1970—a bit stocky and crablike, hirsute, around 5'7", and I just didn't have the tolerance to relate to him as a younger writer who could be a semi-friend to a homosexual poet while letting the poet know I was straight and it didn't make a goddamn bit of difference what folks did behind their doors in th'privacy of their own caves. I mean nine out of ten times I myself climax. I've a member in my right hand. Maybe I'm gay too but just for myself.

Every single time I saw Harold Norse pedaling by, walking by, he was always alone. *This man was a loner.* Absolutely. A very fine quality in my opinion. What else? Oh yes. Several times he took a step or two inside the front door of my Venice Candleshop, as if to just say hello. Maybe I snubbed the man. I can't remember—I don't think I did—I think I'd nod a greeting from the work area in back . . .

I must have irritated him somehow for him to refer to me as a "purple baboon" in his magazine *Bastard Angel #2*. Or was it *#1*? Or *#3*.

I don't know. The least I could have done was act friendly. Well, I guess I was an asshole. A fool. A wax cynic. A womanizer preying upon my customers. Like a spider hanging in there until a correctly shaped female innocently stepped in to fondle my *tree candle erect limbs with a wee little wick, as yet unlit*, "C'mon Baby Light My Fire!"

Jim Morrison came in a few times too. At night I'd often hear him singing from inside the "Cheetah," a Rock Hall at the end of Lick Pier, about half a block north of my shop.

Late 1969 or early 1970:

It's at Harold Norse's Venice Beach apartment I first hear the name "Sylvia Plath." Bukowski, Neeli, and myself have driven three short blocks from my candleshop on Rose to Harold's apartment on Paloma and the Speedway. Speedway is a well traveled alley running parallel to the Venice Boardwalk and about 90 feet east of it. Speedway is right behind my candleshop and the Boardwalk is right in front.

We were going to walk but for some reason I'm driving us three to Harold Norse's place. Bukowski retches out my car's passenger door just before I step on the gas. All three of us are drunk. Bukowski and Neeli had been dipping candles in one of the 55 gallon barrels. I watched them for a few seconds. They were as curious as youngsters in a Crafts Class, both simultaneously dipping and then bending their necks and heads over the top of the barrel. The hot wax is semi-transparent and they were eying their wicks, like a fisherman watching his line underwater.

I walked out on the sand. Bukowski and Neeli were taking care of the candleshop for about ten minutes. When I returned, either Buk or Neeli stated we should now visit Harold Norse. It was decided, and I closed my shop.

Harold Norse had a poster of Rimbaud on his front room wall. His flat was on the second floor of a large rectangular red brick apartment house. Inside his place, several comfy old easy chairs, a nice cushioned sofa one could sink into—Harold's pad was nicely put together. The first book he showed us was a Grove Press (I think) paperback—Norse's translations of an ancient Italian poet, Belli. I'd never heard of Belli but on the back cover it said William Carlos Williams was very excited about Harold Norse's translations of this book.

E.G. Belli's poems—this book passed from hand to hand. When it got to me I tried reading from some of the poetry. It didn't seem to hold me at all. Then I heard Harold talking and the only words I remember in his few sentences were "Sylvia Plath." I remember Bukowski reacted with a muffled kind of "... ummphh ..."

It would be a year or more before I read *Ariel*. Sylvia Plath knocked me over with her *red bone* strength. Anyhow, it was too late to try to meet her, too. Years earlier she'd gassed herself in her kitchen. Damn. I would have enjoyed meeting Sylvia.

The three of us still visiting Norse; Neeli and Bukowski begin talking to each other a bit louder, begin asking one another, perhaps betting whether or not Harold Norse *has a wig on*. "Yes he does . . . Yes HE DOES!!" argues Bukowski as if Harold Norse is now in Greece and not ten feet away. "Ohhh Hank, Harold doesn't wear a wig . . ." says Neeli in his own version of Bukowski's unique drawl. I can't quite believe what I'm hearing from these two fellows. To me their "debate" seems comical/ornery/rude/idiotic/mean-spirited/teasing/belligerent all at once. Harold Norse has a small close-lipped semi-grin. He isn't taking part in this argument between Neeli and Hank—which somehow seems like it's taking place on a stage. Harold Norse then takes care of some chores; he closes some dresser drawers; tidies up his books; lifts up a cardboard box with books inside and walks a few steps and puts it down. All the while, the great wig debate continues.

Suddenly the three of us are outside taking an elevator

down one floor. We've said friendly goodbyes to Norse. It's night, we're out on the Speedway now where I've parked. Nobody's around except us in this extra large alley, our voices echoing against the backsides of brick and stucco three and four story apartment houses.

Harold Norse never tells us for sure whether or not he wears a wig. He was evocative and interested when he talked about Sylvia Plath. I don't remember what he said about her, just how he said it: appreciative, respectful, admiring.

# 26

Let's drive to Hank's Carlton Way flat—about a block southeast of a most revealing Hollywood intersection: Western Avenue and Hollywood Boulevard.

It's around 2:00 P.M. and sunny. Hank's flat is on the north side of little Carlton Way. It's a gray bunch of apartments here, old duplexes. Hank's is the second up on the right. One walks up a few steps to the first level with an apartment on either side, then I believe a few more steps and here are the second two-story set of flats. Hank's has a five by eight porch area. All these buildings are two stories, about a dozen flats in all. Hank has covered the large windows which open on the porch itself, to the right of his front door.

I think about those white sheets as I approach. Against the solid gray stucco walls these white sheets really stand out. An area about five feet high and seven feet wide is fully covered by white sheets, sheets being inside the glass. It's like a GIANT SURRENDER SIGN: this interpretation hits me and lasts about nine seconds. Why would I think that?

Several years earlier I'd been honored to have a little preface of sorts in the front of *Confessions* . . . One of my sentences, excerpted from my letter to Doug Blazek, went:

> . . . THIS MAN IS A MAN! THIS MAN
> IS PRESIDENT OF MY AMERICA! . . .

And now for a longish nine seconds I'm thinking MY PRESIDENT has or is surrendering, waving his white bed-sheet flag. Maybe there's something wrong with me. It must be.

More likely it's only that Bukowski needs his privacy. But other sheets could have accomplished this. Nonsense! Hank's white tee-shirts keep his privacy too, and paradoxically are a kind of Victory Sign as he graces along sidewalks, etc. But these white sheets seem different. His tee-shirts are *happy white*.

(Now my conscience speaks aloud, midnight, 7/19/94: "I don't know, I must be crazy.")

I'm at his front door. Directly to my right is the wall with big windows. I mean his front door wall is at a right angle to his bedroom wall. There is a screen door in front of the door—his De Longpre pad had no front screen door. Hank opens his front door and for a second or two we eye each other through screen. I'm facing it straight on and he's sort of half facing me and half the right door jamb, but he is looking to his right at me. His chin is a slight inch bowed down, and he is almost peeking at me. He seems somewhat down, like he's a bit bluer here than in his old De Longpre lair. His old place was up front and this cave is a couple back on the right and has another flat right on top of it. Maybe th'tenant upstairs has been jumping up and down?

Now I know what it is about those sheets! The sun is shining flat out on them. It's afternoon and the sun is hitting them because th'sun is still high enough in th'west to beam straight at a 45 degree angle east and downward to blast straight on Hank's bedroom windows, which face west . . . WHITE SO WHITE BLINDING WHITE.

And I'm wearing dark glasses; if I'd arrived an hour later, there'd be no white blinding bed-sheet memory in me.

Hank is behind the screen door standing and looking at me at an angle, 45 degrees to his right, also. Well, Hank is th'sun with both sun and Hank shining/eying/expressing at th'same exact angle. It's OK with me.

In seconds I'll be inside and see a large cardboard box on his floor, in th'midst of his front room. It will be filled to its brim with big thick brand new paperback books, all the same book, maybe 50 new "author's copies" of *Factotum*. I take a seat on his old sofa and I look and look at this box of new tomes, Hank's just-birthed fiction, and as I almost stare at this box a single medium-size cockroach crawls up from inside and balances along the rim of the box that's closest to me; then it casually climbs straight down the outside of this box. This does not seem a good omen to me.

## 27

*Just took a teacup half full of wild birdseed out and lifted it up to th'7 foot high shelf and spilled their supper, and now I'm sure Aphrodite's doves (who coo in th'fig tree for this kind of breakfast—and sparrows and finches too) are eating.*

*My readers, please, get some wild birdseed, feed th'little fuckers. Make sure cats will have a tough time approaching them. Don't tell anybody of your good deeds, don't be like me. Mr. Christ had it right: bragging of good deeds lessens th'worth, turns it to slime.*

Bukowski as Christ? Job? Nobody asked. Back in his De Longpre cave, I was sneaking a peek into his dark bedroom. The door was open. Bedroom door. I'd just taken a beer leak and before I'd entered the bathroom I looked to my left through the open bedroom door. No lights on in there, 90% darkened, 10% visible enough to make out his double bed, white sheets twisted almost in knots and seemingly tossed and swirled in high emotional *EH WHO GIVES A FUCK WHAT I DO WITH MY DAMN SHEETS!*

My first impression was that his bedroom looked like that of a big-big-problems alcoholic. His front room was straightened and I guess I wasn't supposed to be glimpsing his bedroom that night. But the door was open and only about five feet to my left as I entered his bathroom. I got a two second initial glimpse.

Entered bathroom and closed bathroom door. Hank had gone into his bathroom before I first did this and I noticed he had shut his bathroom door behind him so I shut the door behind me. I pissed/urinated/leaked/pee-ed/then looked at myself in smallish mirror above sink and exited bathroom and looked to my right for a second glimpse into his dark bedroom. This time I saw something new.

In the dark I barely could make it out. I was drunk, therefore relaxed. I could hesitate as I stood in front of bathroom door. An intoxicated man had more of an excuse to stand still and weave in inner space for awhile. What I saw was a second set of concrete blocks and bricks holding shelves and hundreds more books and magazines on the shelves, almost identical to those books/mags/shelves in Hank's front room. I figured that those mags/books Hank kept in his bedroom were extra private publications, perhaps.

The rest of his bedroom objects and sheets and blankets and whatever these things were, were tossed and hurled about in what appeared a *chaotic mess. Order* in th'front room—well lit *order.*

*Chaos* in his bedroom/darkened/lights-off-unlit *chaos.* I didn't take any steps closer to the bedroom door; it was wide open but it was obvious to me I would be stepping over his *privacy line* if I'd taken even one step to my right instead of moving my body straight ahead into his front room again. It seemed OK for me to *look right* but *not move an inch right.*

## 28

Hank and I attacked each other in our writings, quite a bit. Flattery is dull. It's nice to read it and then you forget it. Flattery can uplift the hell out of one. Advice is better than flattery but only when it's requested. I'm always pushing advice on folks who haven't asked. Once I advised Bukowski to write books more like *The Days Run Away Like Wild Horses Over the Hills* and less like *Factotum*. I remember it well, th'look on his face when I said that: disappointed. He was a tiny bit chagrined and very silent and disappointed, as he sort of backed up from me at an angle to my left. He's backing up and his face is darker reddish.

It's my second visit to his Carlton Way place. Night. He's alone. He's just let me in. My first visit was a few weeks or month ago when I was almost blinded by white bed sheets in his window. When I left I was holding a gift from Hank: *Factotum*.

I took it home and began reading, stopped at the second and third paragraph when I came to "... cardboard suitcase ..."

Some Hamsun book, perhaps *Wandering* or *Wanderers* or whatever it is, had our hero Knut or Jurgen or whoever he was, adventuring through Norway with his cardboard suitcase. I'd just finished reading it, enjoying it, when I began *Factotum*. So I skimmed *Factotum*. It seemed to include many of Hank's pieces that I'd read years earlier in *Confessions* . . .. and *All the*

*Assholes . . .* and in underground newspapers.

Here I was face to face with Hank, telling him, criticizing his just published *Factotum*. In his own cave I was (well, I just said it aloud to myself) fucking up.

"I was fucking up. No wonder he attacked me. I deserved to be attacked."

Honest arrogance may be better than hypocritical humility. Even if I was correct about *Factotum* I still deserved Hank's attack.

# 29

Today I opened *Screams from the Balcony* for a moment. The first line I read was Bukowski saying Patchen's writing was a little "too sugary for me."

I mean in one short sentence Bukowski characterizes another scribe's whole lifetime body of work, and makes it stick.

Patchen was very strong. He taught me much—how to put two words together for spice: "pigpiss" for example. Without Patchen, I never would have written "pigpiss."

Too sugary? As soon as Hank wrote me this, it became true for myself also. But Patchen was one of the strongest bravest scribes I came across in the mid-sixties. In one of his books, perhaps *Memoirs of a Shy Pornographer*, you would turn open both front and back covers and see maybe 65 different blurbs about Patchen's writings, 65 different critics' comments, all SLAMS! It was delightful to read all of 'em. I loved Patchen, never knew him, never wrote him, but I loved his *Love Poems* published by City Lights, *Pocket Poets Series*, purple and white cover, a wonderful thing; *Love Poems by Kenneth Patchen* from City Lights Publishers: is it still available?

And none of these chapters would be around if it weren't for a blend of encouragement, tolerance, and vital advice given me by David Garcia, John Martin, Douglas Goodwin, Jeffrey H. Weinberg, Marvin Malone, and Al Berlinski. Bless your wonderful kind alive warm and generous husbands' asses!

   I'm single. I've followed Bukowski's sound advice he spoke through telephone to me, wrote me distinctly and succinctly said to me in person:

> ah, Steve, the FEMALE. there is no way. don't wait for the good woman. she doesn't exist. there are women who can make you feel more with their bodies and their souls but these are the exact women who will turn the knife into you right in front of the crowd. of course, I expect this, but the knife still cuts. the female loves to play man against man. and if she is in a position to do it there is not one who will not resist. the male, for all his bravado and exploration, is the loyal one, the one who generally feels love. the female is skilled at betrayal. and torture and damnation. never envy a man his lady. behind it all lays a living hell. I know you're not going to quit the chase, but when you go into it, for Christ's sake, realize that you are going to be burned ahead of time. never go in totally *open*. the madhouses and skidrows are full of those. remember, the female is any man's woman at any time. the choice is hers. and she's going to rip the son of a bitch she goes to just like she ripped you. but never hate the woman. understand that she is channeled this way and let her go. solitude too brings a love as tall as the mountains. fuck the skies. amen.
>
> (Nov. 5, 1971)

   That Charles Bukowski paragraph in a letter he sent me in 1971, more than anything else by a million goddamn miles, has kept me alive somewhat to the chagrin of Aphrodite herself. She expressly insinuated to me I should have fallen in a snowbank and frozen to death for love of her, ala the young brutish industrialist in D. H. Lawrence's *Women In Love*.

This was the same time I was writing those 300 nauseating odes that Hank comments on in his own poem, "300 Poems," published in *Mockingbird Wish Me Luck*. So Hank saved my ass on the one hand and stuck his epee up it on the other hand.

Yes sir, that's how it happened. I know, because it's my ass.

# 30

It's that time during the 1960's Hank is hooked up with a woman artist, Linda King, and now it's night, about 8:00 P.M. or so and someone is knocking at my door and I open and there're Hank, Linda, and another woman. Hank is waiting to come in with two women. I let'em all in here and soon I'm told this other gal is Linda King's sister.

I'm told this sister is a real estate broker/agent. She does have a kind of self-assured/straight air about her. She seems confident, pleasantly attractive, about 30, and Hank has brought a sixpack or two along. We open up beers and drink happily. This is the first time Hank has visited with two women.

After awhile we are pretty high and while Hank is in the bathroom, I walk a few steps to where Linda's sister is standing, this location being about ten feet from where I now type this sheet. And I place my hand lightly upon her sweater at her left breast and she *does not protest.* I'm looking into her eyes from about six inches away. I'm about to kiss her, I suppose, when Hank suddenly opens the bathroom door and sees what she and I are up to. He sees my hand on her sweater at her breast and he blurts semi-loudly and warningly, "UH OH! NO NO NO . . . HEY HEY . . ."

And I look to my right at him and see that he's sort of shocked and almost pissed and stern in face. I remove my hand from Linda's sister's chest and I move back a foot or two. I think to myself, what the hell is with Hank? Is he some Puritan or something? What th'hell did he bring her along for if I can't feel her and maybe kiss her? After all, I only feel like kissing about one out of one thousand women I meet!

Years later I'll read something by Bukowski in which he says his own sexual attitudes are rather *puritanical.*

No kidding! He will also state his sexual feelings are perhaps those of a prude. No shit!

How did Linda's sister react to Bukowski's sudden displeasure at my own claw upon her breast? Matter of factly.

A month or so after this visit described above, I am conversing with Hank at his place or my place, and he speaks of Linda's sister as being a woman who probably knows more about life than most folks, in that she works hard at selling real estate and she has done so for many years, and thus knows how to survive in present-day society more than all others who don't work seriously at a conventional past-time.

**31**

I'm not sure if it was right after he moved out of De Longpre, or Carlton Way. For several months he took an apartment on Oxford Street somewhere around Sixth and Normandy, I believe. This was a truly awful cage.

This Oxford apartment was about the most lifeless, sad, pathetic, prison-like living quarters I'd ever seen. One of his women had rented the place for him. Maybe it was to await the preparation of his eventual San Pedro house. I don't know.

It was a sunny day in L.A. But hazy. An opaque haze, hard to look at. What an ugly fucking town this is. Why is it once when I was in Hawaii I couldn't wait to get back to my birthplace, L.A.? When I first saw the brown clot of urban miasma/air below me from my airplane window, why is it I felt so good to be home?

Hank asked me to visit his place on Oxford. I drove over one day about noon. Oxford is a side street but seems as wide as a freeway. It must be eight car lanes wide. I drove south on Oxford looking for his new address. Both sides of the street had monolithic apartment houses, all shaped in squares. I mean each apartment house had about 50 units and each unit was a square glued to the next unit or above and below other squares, all gray or beige, no greenery. Maybe there were a few tiny patches of grass but these sparse patches accentuated the lack of vegetation rather than alleviated it.

What nightmarish hatred of a man could cause a supposed friend of his to rent him such a place in such a monstrous so called "neighborhood"?

Uh?

I know it was a woman. Hank told me it was a woman who arranged for him to move into this area. I'm not sure which woman. It, rather she, might have been Linda King, or his future wife, or Liza. I can't remember. Whoever it was, was surely mete-ing out revenge and punishment to Charles Bukowski.

The reader might wonder why Steve Richmond, self-proclaimed pal of Charles Buk, why I myself did not help Hank rent a finer lair?

That's easy. I was a feckless asshole, self absorbed, occupied catching th'clap seven times from th'noble young women who bathed at Venice Beach, strolled Venice Boardwalk, habituated th'lively butcher and baker and candlestick maker shops on th'Boardwalk. I happened to be th'*candlemaker*. I was too busy satisfying and then satiating my young savage needs, way too busy to look around for a temporary pad for Charles Bukowski.

So it is noon and I'm driving south on Oxford Street about three miles west of downtown L.A., the street wide as a freeway. My car is the only moving thing on Oxford; there are no other vehicles, no human beings anywhere in sight, no vegetation, just huge wall to wall structures on either side of me, square heaped upon prison-like square. I can understand why no cars, no people, no busses, no taxis, no vegetation even is visible to me: they all have better places to be.

On my right I finally spot Bukowski's address. It's the gray face of industrial death in America, a developer's happy dream; a multi-dwelling structure where 100% primary focus has been rental income per square inch of habitation space, not living space. Nobody could live inside, nor even around or outside, that kind of building.

This place is fucking sun-haze-hell—the street, the

building, everything, the whole fucking area. Such are my thoughts as I park.

There are no parking signs. One can park his car here forever I guess. No other cars parked on Oxford Street. What a fucking pit.

I'm trudging up at least 100 cement steps along the left side of stucco square white beige or maybe gray units. A 50 to 100 square upon square apartment house on Oxford Street or Avenue or whatever, located near Wilshire and Vermont or Normandy about three miles west of downtown L.A.

Surreal. Because there are perhaps 1,000 or more living units within a radius of one block to my body and not one single living thing is visible—traffic noise way off in distance—but not an ant or mouse or bird, certainly no human around save myself, trudging up seven or nine stairs then several level steps, then seven to nine steps on up and up and to the very back wall of this apartment square-shaped three or four story stucco prison fortress.

Hank's apartment is the very back one. I enter a vertical rectangle opening of shadow, an outer short hall, find his front door and knock or ring. He opens up. He's *dejected*, a wee bit of apathy in his face. He beckons me in and he immediately does an about face and steps one pace forward, turns left and takes a few more paces, then he plops down on the sofa—chintz sofa. I take a chair and look at his face: *dejected.* He looks at me without saying anything. No need at all for him to talk. He looks at me and his face is a kind of facial shrug as if WHAT THE HELL CAN I DO? BECAUSE I'M HERE NOW AND THIS PLACE IS JUST AS IT OBVIOUSLY APPEARS TO YOU AND WHAT CAN I DO NOW?

He's a trapped King Lion in a back forget-all-about-it cage at some zoo which no one wishes to name because this zoo is a disgrace.

He doesn't say anything for the first few minutes. There is just dejection in his face, a wee bit of sadness mixed with irony, a slight winsome smile at lip corners but altogether he communicates via his face that he had been HAD. Actually, his apartment is not so bad inside. It's a typical small semi-modern apartment interior.

He then explains that he's here for a few months while another lair is being prepared. Probably he means his coming San Pedro home, but it could be he refers to his Carlton Way flat in East Hollywood. I just don't remember this particular. I do recall him telling me that this Oxford place is not so hot for writing. Either he can't write at all here or he is writing very very little.

Ah well, he'll be out of here in a few months. Paradoxically, this place is an unlikely hideaway. This place is way beyond anyone's imagination. I visit for about 20 minutes. Our talk is very quiet, just an exchange of some literary info I can't begin to remember. He is somewhat disconsolate about having to remain in there as I make my farewells. He knows every time he leaves he will have to walk up a hundred horrifying stairs upon his return.

# 32

Bukowski once brought a woman here to visit whom he then married and lived with right up to his passing away.

Linda B.*

She was quiet and well-mannered and I felt she was the woman for Bukowski. I told him so. I think he brought her along sometime in 1983 or so, two years before their marriage. I think he brought her here to see what my feelings about her would be.

Why else would be bring along Linda, THE Linda he would marry? I think on *Burning In Water Drowning In Flame.* Linda's Scorpio, fixed water. Hank is Leo, sun, fixed fire. Linda is drowning in him and he burning in her.

Once Hank begins his life with Linda B. his friendship and interactions with myself are very much decreased. I've met her, he has brought her to visit here in my cave once. She is quiet and strong and lovely and more than just "seems" to be with him, love him; and I soon advise Hank that this is a good woman for him, to mate with, to be with, to marry if he wishes. I know I told him I felt she is a fine woman for him. I can't believe my advice has any real influence on him.

I do not feel resentful at all of her. There is no feeling at all in me that she is somehow taking Hank away from me as a pal. If I do have such inner feelings these feelings are utterly unknown by my consciousness.

I am happy for him. He needs a right woman because he

*Linda Lee Beighle, future wife

112

needs a woman to live with and care for him. Otherwise, he's prone to falling drunk-passed-out-on-his-floor and laying there for three days and nights.

I believe this woman Linda B. is Hank's right mate right up until about 30 seconds after I open and enter Siam West Restaurant that day in 1985—their wedding reception—and she walks up to greet me and she says some words which absolutely change my whole idea of her. These words she says to me most likely are innocent teasing of me. She says "There are no demons here, Steve."

## 33

I'm at Bukowski's front door at his East Hollywood apartment on Carlton Way. The time is late afternoon or just after sundown. Now I remember the time as around 7:30 P.M. and his front door is really two doors, an outer screen door and then the normal wooden front door. The inner wood door is open wide and I am peering through the closed screen door.

I have not called ahead. I am visiting him unannounced just as he has recently visited my cave unannounced. I remember now that most likely he has come and opened his inner wood door to my knocks. He has then greeted me through the screen door and he then has walked back into his apartment front room to say something to a woman who I see back near his kitchen. Both Bukowski and this woman inside his cave are wearing black silk Chinese happy gowns. These gowns are called "Love Kimonos" or something like this.

Lovers buy these kimonos in His and Her pairs and these kimonos are short as miniskirts. These kimonos are cut so that the bottoms are just above one's knees.

The black satin or silk love kimonos which Bukowski and his lover—this gal is Bukowski's obvious lover/woman; I can tell easily by how he and she are almost giggling together, so happy and jolly, so playful as pure lovers—these kimonos are black silk, and embroidered flowers scatter upon these gowns, so that I see through the outer screen door . . . I see a pair of

114

100% happy lovers.

I think right then that no way am I going to enter through this unlocked screen door into the interior of Bukowski's cave there on Carlton Way and no way am I going now to interrupt whatsoever this pair of *pure happy love birds.* I feel great for Bukowski at that moment because it is the happiest moment re romantic love that I have ever witnessed. His woman has a wonderful smile and she too is in a romantic delight. How can I walk in and disrupt such a superb time they are experiencing? There would be absolutely no way that I might increase their happiness. I could only hurt their present happiness, cheerful sharing of the best of each other. That is what I was thinking as I stood there. That is why I then said through the screen, *"Carry on! Carry on! I shall see you all later! Adios . . ."*

I said this, or something near this. The woman with Bukowski was to become Linda Bukowski. That few minutes I stood there at his front door was the most happy I ever saw Bukowski with a woman. A pair of happy true "love birds." I was thinking too how rare it was to see a pair of folks like this who were not kids, but who were as happy as young lovers. I also remember a pang of envy, envy that I was not then in such a sort of love with a woman, myself.

I walked back out to Carlton Way. I don't remember any more.

**34**

Ports O' Call restaurant area at San Pedro Harbor, Los Angeles. It's summer 1985—Bukowski's wedding day. It will be the last time I will see Hank in person, alive.

I'm invited to the wedding reception, not the earlier ceremony. I haven't seen Hank for a few years, since around 1982, I believe. He has written a good number of letters to me, but he writes he feels he would be "invading" somehow if he visits here at my cave. I feel the same way about barging in on him at his San Pedro home.

A Thai Cafe named "Siam West" on the waterfront of San Pedro Harbor. Tables in a big dining room and tables out on an adjoining wooden terrace over the water. This outside terrace supported by telephone-pole-like piling driven into the sand. Inner harbor water depth about ten feet I guess, where the terrace outer railing is.

But I haven't even gone in the goddamn place yet. I've been walking around the lanes of this area: cafes, shops, and curio shops and more restaurants, crowded as Ports O' Call crowds can get. Gigantic parking lots out there, packed with what seems thousands of American Middle Class chariots; Whites and Latinos and a few Blacks—thousands jamming Ports O' Call area this Sunny As Fucking Hell Sunday afternoon.

So I'm on my way walking down and back and forth along lanes, getting a feel of Ports O' Call. Now I'm nearing

Linda Lee Beighle
and
Charles Bukowski
are very happy to
request the honour of your presence
at the celebration of their marriage
at a Buffet-Reception
Sunday, the eighteenth of August
nineteen hundred and eighty-five
at three o'clock in the afternoon
at Siam West
Ports O'Call
San Pedro, California

"Siam West." There is a small but sturdy self-standing sign made of heavy wood, and this sign stands about seven feet out from "Siam West's" front door. The removable letters posted on this sign say something like

PRIVATE PARTY TODAY
Wedding Reception for Linda & Hank Bukowski

I walk past this heavily made self-standing bulletin sign of sorts and get to the front door, a heavily made, somewhat ornate door. I have no idea what the hell I'm going to see or who I'm going to meet when I pull this front door open or push it open.

My gut is acting up. My stomach is queasy. I'm plain shit-nervous.

Well, I open the door and step inside.

It's a big panorama I see in this "Siam West." My eyes start at far left and sweep slow right, like a camera. At left are a few oriental-seeming cooks, food preparers, about 40 feet away from me, working in a kind of open-to-view kitchen area. Spits and barbecues and fiery grill, etc.

I see first a man standing right under the open skylight area and sun rays—broken fine rays of not too bright sunlight—put his standing body-being in a kind of "spotlight," natural sun-spotlight *for me,* for my eyes as I look a bit to my right of center at him standing there, Zen-like in his well-being and peace He is obviously a happy and realized fellow. He wears a suit, tie, glasses, has a full beard, is standing with his arms angled straight down in front of him so his hands are folded a bit together down about at his waist or a bit below. Quite natural, a good mannered way to stand. Quiet. Slight smile. This is a *complete man.*

Then I recognize him. He's about 35 feet from me in rays of sunlight, muted rays just right light. He is John Martin. Haven't seen him for maybe ten whole years! Last time I saw him was at his Black Sparrow Press office in West L.A. off Motor Avenue, when I refused to shake his hand! I was pissed off.

Boy, he looks good standing there.

*Uh oh. I'm being approached by a woman in a beige old-time wedding dress, and a large floppy antique kind of hat.*

Linda Bukowski walked up to me and said "THERE ARE NO DEMONS HERE, STEVE."

My stomach was sour and I was feeling sickly, and so perhaps took her words and her appearance to me and everything else about her that I sensed at the moment—I perhaps took it all as black and foreboding and even evil as possible.

However, it certainly did appear to me and seem to me right then, that Linda now felt freed of having to appear as the epitome of *the good woman, the perfect woman for Charles Bukowski.*

Now she felt free to say what she felt like saying, be who she really felt she wished to be . . . because that morning the legal wedding ceremony had been done, because now she was indeed Mrs. or Ms. Charles Bukowski, and if anybody at all, including myself, didn't like it . . . well, tough luck.

I wasn't thinking anything whatsoever near nor about in any way *demons* as I stood there. Rather, I was hoping this would be a fine warm celebration, and I would feel wonderful, and Hank and Linda would feel great, and all the hundred or so guests would have a terrific time, and that would be that.

Hank had bought a fine house on a hill above L.A. Harbor and he bought a new English sports car for his new wife, and when he walked near the table I sat at during the reception he stated clear and in mock serious/jest, *"You better like all this food and drink because I'm paying for it!"*

He sort of said this to all of us guests as a group whole. And we did like it, th'finest and tastiest Thai sweetmeats and shellfish and all th'bloody booze we desired and a great Reggae Quartet or Octet to hear and dance all we wished, if we wished to dance. Ten or fifteen grand at least is what that "Siam West" restaurant must have cost him for a whole Sunday afternoon. He liked making money from his writings. It made him a King, a grand rich King.

I don't remember feeling envious that day at the reception. I remember wishing he didn't have to seem to be playing a glorious and packed-with-life old Greek Sage and Lover and Rascal and Dancer and Lover and *Lover and White Suited*—because I wanted him to be himself. *Himself* seemed so fine enough. He was being Zorba the Greek and I loved the real Charles Bukowski. It was a come-down for him, it seemed to me.

Why was he doing it? It didn't make any sense to me. I could tell he was uneasy doing this, even if I was the only one. Even if I was dead wrong, I could still tell he was acting the old Greek fisherman-lover and lover and soulful folk hero dancer and white suited spirit of LifeLifeLifeLifeLife. But Charles Bukowski as his real self *had more life than anyone*. Even Zorba th'Greek.

Well, there I was at the big round table on the wood balcony of "Siam West" and sunny it was, and great Reggae music played, and Buk danced like Zorba, full of magic energy, showing us young farts how a real man celebrates a marriage of *strong raw poem making authentic art maker*. I mean he was enjoying himself and had more Greek god energy than all us 100 guests put together.

And I looked at the guests getting drunker more and more, and I myself was drunker, and all I saw I really didn't want to be seeing very much, so I stood up and sneaked out of Siam West just as the cake was to be sliced.

And nobody saw me walking out. And I got to the front door of Siam West and opened it, and moved through into *a whole other reality*. And I felt better, less trapped now, freer, not under the constraints of acting correct and civil at Charles Bukowski's Wedding Reception Party.

121

Demons? Hell no. Demons were as far away from my spirit as my cave some 20 miles north of San Pedro Harbor and Ports O' Call restaurant area and Siam West Thai Cafe. Fuck Demons! They were nowhere around this beautiful celebration of Earth's best poet and his new wife and this unique day of their splendid and special matrimony. Demons? Why should Linda even say such a word? And just hours after saying *"I do."*

# 35

What happened after 1969 to influence Bukowski to begin reading at universities?

Did Bukowski's writing change at all beginning around 1970? Did he cease writing how he detested "the rich?"

Did he cease writing how folks who owned and drove Cadillacs were dead?

Did he stop writing about owners of apartment houses as "landlords full of maggots?"

Did he even just "tone it down" a little?

Did he begin writing that endurance is more important than the truth?

Did he cease writing and/or telephoning me with sincere apologies about something he did the night before while we were drinking together? Yes. Did he show up here knocking and when I opened the door did he ask three visits in a row, "Can I take a shit?"

Did he write a Foreword to my vanity published book titled *Earth Rose* in the year 1974? Yes.

Did he begin flying all over the damn country reading at university after public auditorium after museum auditorium for $500 plus round-trip airfare? Yes.

Until his death in 1994 was he still our planet's finest scribe by 99 miles? I think Yes.

Why did he change in 1970? What happened in 1969-

1970 which got him acting, doing things, doing such opposing things to ideals he clearly espoused in his works between 1965 to 1969? Maybe the year 1965 is too late. Maybe he actually lived these earlier ideals from 1955 to 1969. Maybe I state the year "1965" only because that's the year that "I" first met him and got to know him as a close friend and mentor, in my opinion.

("Who the fuck knows?" is what I just cynically muttered out loud. Maybe I just said this too clear to be called a "mutter.")

So many *MAYBES.*

I know I never bitched to him about these above supposed "changes." In fact I often wrote words such as, *"Bukowski deserves every material reward he is getting and will ever get for his unequaled works. "* I really believed this. Part of me still believes this. Maybe 99% of me.

Between 1965 and 1969 Bukowski apologized to me around ten different times. Not even once had he done anything at all which called for his apology to myself. I even began wondering why he was sincerely apologizing to me so often for things he hadn't done or said. He would tell me he was so drunk he couldn't remember. I guess he was making sure.

## 36

What did Bukowski feel about writing for money? In one of his earliest letters, he writes me that it doesn't work. Writing something for money does not work. It will be dead on arrival. He writes me this message in 1966, I believe.

Six or seven years later I am reading an issue of *The Berkeley Barb* and there's a Buk story on its front page. He's quoted as bellowing something like, *"I'm a whore for th'highest bidder!"*

During the Spring of 1994 I get an odd impulse to telephone John Martin's office, ask him what I should do about *90 Minutes of Hell*, a two record album of Bukowski reading around fifty odes and one short story.

During this conversation Martin refers to his first meeting with Bukowski as, ". . . the day Rolls met Royce."

In 1988 I edit and publish *Stance Magazine #5*. Inside is a Buk ode which includes his line about being pleased as he opens some German magazine; he's pleased his published short story is in German because he doesn't even have to read it. Why is he pleased he doesn't have to read it? Is it written more for the money than the honor?

Of course he wants/needs money for his writings. All through *Screams from the Balcony* he over and over in letter after letter celebrates in his blasé manner various amounts of money paid him by his growing number of publishers. He emphasized in these letters how he needed such payments to pay child support and more days than not at the track. He needed money for his gals and one day in the seventies Ben Pleasants told me Bukowski told him that when Buk's bank account got down to a minimum of $20,000.00 Bukowski began to worry. Seriously worry. He felt insecure when his reserves decreased to twenty grand.

Beer expense was the main bill when Bukowski and I would meet and share time. He paid about three-quarters of our mutual beer expenses and he drank about two-thirds of our total hundred sixpacks or so.

What did Bukowski feel about making money from his writings? He felt goddamn fucking good. Good enough to pay $25,000.00 cash all in a lump for his first new car, a black BMW two-door model 633 or 635 point something or other, the most gorgeous and classiest BMW of that year, 1978 or so, and he wrote many a stanza how he raced it on th'Pasadena Freeway and loved doing it and knew he was an idiot doing this but fuck it, it was simply *great fun*!

**37**

Back in '88 Hank had written me and told me to check him out whenever I needed to. I wrote a few times. He wrote back. I heard he was sick. Suddenly, after months of no writing, I wrote him again with the message I was coming in two days to check him out. The day my letter would have arrived, Hank died (I was told). I was about to check him out two days after my letter arrived. Death knew I would blow th'plan. Death decided let's do it now before Richmond messes it all up!

Something doesn't seem to make sense to me. Or something makes all too good sense to me: that Buk just couldn't handle the fan pressure, the incessant *signing requests.* So, I hope he is still alive and writing under the pen-name Two Ton Tony.

Why do I go on like this? Comrades often assure me Hank has passed on. Perhaps my reasoning is based on the multiple times Hank communicated to me his main wish as far as longevity—to live to the year 2000 and celebrate his 80th birthday on August 16, 2000. I had written him it was my wish to host and treat him and his pals on that date for what was to be one wonderful hell of an 80th Birthday Party.

**38**

I suppose I was angry because it seemed to me I was kept away from Hank's funeral. I had called Red* at his bookshop and he told me that it was a secret as to the location of Hank's funeral and I felt that Bukowski's closest relations did not want me there. I was angry at all those *close to Bukowski* during his last years. I was blaming all of them for squeezing Hank of his juices, etc. I was afraid that I would make some scene if I attended his funeral. I'd heard a rumor that the week before his death some mistake had taken place during a transfusion of blood he was receiving at some hospital. I had heard some needle connection slipped out or some mistake or accident occurred which should have been immediately fixed by an attending nurse but that the nurse was out of the room and that Hank really took a downward turn when this happened and never recovered.

I don't know if this is fact or horseshit untrue rumor.

No family member called me to tell me of Hank's last rites. They apparently did not want me there. I figured maybe Hank didn't want me there. Hank was, in his last years, much closer to Sean Penn. Sean Penn and his bodyguards were there. Anyhow, I didn't want to see any of those people who I felt had squeezed Hank of his vital life juices, vital creative juices, and if I completely was wrong about my feelings it wouldn't surprise me.

*Sholom "Red" Stodolsky

128

Editors of major newspapers across America got the wrong idea about Bukowski, namely that he was "King Of The Beatniks." This was their way of diminishing his incomparable body of work. Less luck to all those stinking Editors, Academics, Snide Bastards, Abominable Staid Safe Castrated Mannikins Locked, Securely Up In Their Ivory Towers Of Drek. Hmm, yes, terrible people who haven't answered my multiple cards and letters. Silence is the best weapon. They are my enemies. SNOBS. Of course, often I'd get pissed off at Hank. But he always answered until th'end.

"But it was mostly the photos of your drawings, paintings . . ." writes Hank to me in a letter dated "Sunday, 1965." He tells the reason, the main reason he is inviting me over for a first visit, a first meeting: he digs my artwork. It is my drawings and paintings rather than my writings that he likes. This made good sense to me in 1965 because I'd been only writing for a year or two. I'd been charcoal drawing for more than five years.

Over the last 30 or 40 years Charles Bukowski created thousands of drawings and paintings. For my eye, his drawings and paintings jump with life and unique gift/talent/wonderful coloring.

**39**

Bukowski is still alive.

Hank is in Viareggio, Tripoli, Amsterdam, Ubeda, Paris, Heidelberg . . . Hank is in every town in Germany. Hank is alive, and no need to sign *Charles Bukowski* even once. No need to sign for the swarms of collectors, amateur scribes, publishers, bookshop owners, people, human earth people of all kinds, pleading for just a postcard.

You know those bald Zen guys in orange robes? Give 'em a hundred bucks and they'll do whatever you ask. Please put 160 pounds of elongated weight in a coffin, spread it like a man corpse, bury it six feet under, and don't worry about those 40 attending arty looking folks. They're all so nervous of each other they won't even have a clue what's knocking around inside th'simple pine casket.

Here's a hundred for you, Siddhartha Lao Honeycomb. Here's one hundred for you Steppenwolf Love Zenbashi. Here you are Hesse Mao Hanoi Blue Rose. And I haven't forgotten you Lovely Maiden Savantha Star Star. Now you know what to do. Very good. Hank wishes to have me thank each of you from the bottom of his enduring heart.

**40**

November 15, 1994. BBC pair of film makers visited to interview me about Bukowski. They tell me they're making a 50 minute film documentary about him for British folks, sort of to introduce Bukowski a bit more thoroughly to their countrypersons because now that he has passed away . . . well, I don't quite understand why now instead of a few years ago. They told me Bukowski is still not that "hot" in England. Germany, of course, is Buk Country. Young German girls working in cafes around here, each one of them, answer without hesitation when I mention Charles Bukowski to them. They know him well, they sort of wrinkle up their cheeks and foreheads, they respond to my statement "He was a kind of radical masculinist." They then answer me with this:

"That's for sure!"

As if they actually resent Bukowski for his writings re WOMAN. But they also certainly have respect for his work in their responses. And, they *ALL* know Buk and his work—I mean *ALL THE YOUNG GORGEOUS GERMAN WOMEN WORKING AROUND HERE AS SEMI-TRENDY CAFE HOSTESSES AND WAITRESSES.*

Vanessa, attractive young woman from BBC. Sam, young man from BBC. They are deep into Bukowski.

They laughed most when I related Hank's three consecutive visits here, unexpected, about ten days between each visit, and he asking an identical question each time I opened my front door. It is around 1978.

Someone is knocking.

I walk to my front door and open it and there is Bukowski.

He says first, "Eh, can I take a shit?"

Without hesitation I motion him in and he knows where my head is and he walks right to it and I suppose defecates. He comes out and thanks me; we talk for a minute or two, and he says something like "Well, my Volks is ready at Bug Builders. Gotta go pick it up. You hang in now, kid." And he's gone.

Identical knock and absolutely identical words ten days later. My response is similar but a bit more a mix of guarded irony. He shits, I guess, comes out and leaves soon. Some other errand calls him to accomplish it.

Identical knock and absolutely identical words ten days later. Three strikes he is out. I answer, "Try Chevron up the block." He goes away with a wise old man's subtle smirk.

The BBC couple laughed loud when I told them all this. Then Vanessa asked why I think Bukowski did that. Hmmm.

I explained to her this was Bukowski's way of *SHITTING ON ME* because he must have been angry with me for one thing or another. It may have been he was pissed because I allowed Linda King to come in one early morn at 2:00 A.M., and that I didn't bar her and say, "Oh, you're only trying to make Buk jealous; I ain't going to let you get away with it; *SCRAM LADY.*"

Maybe Bukowski was pissed at me for something else.

This story, true story, seemed to be exactly what Vanessa and Sam were trying to get out of me. They told me a four person film crew is coming in two weeks and I will get $200 for my participation.

Vanessa asked nine out of ten questions. Her questions

revealed much about how Charles Bukowski is thought about-felt-about-etc. in England. And English young intelligentsia. Yes yes yes yes . . .

What Vanessa and Sam did here, was what they drove here—with Vanessa in th'driver's seat—a Probe. Sam made a crack when they got back in the Probe, "Next time we'll do *THE STEVE RICHMOND STORY.*" I guess he thought I was an ego-maniac . . . snide motherfucker.

I'm almost nervous. I'm new at a film crew, being recorded. What do I do with my damn hands? I don't give a fuck—(I just said that phrase aloud)—I'm a pillar of literary subtlety, who does not give a - - - I mean is 53 years old and feels like a - - -, I mean Hank advised me, even ordered me, YOU AREN'T GOING TO BE A TV POET, ARE YOU?

Then a few years went by and I saw him on TV and then on TV again. But I was told today, rather yesterday, in a phone call from an English gal who "I call the day before"—she told me this docu-film won't be shown in th'USA.

I responded, "Yeah this country censors out anything that's alive."

Which wasn't true, but . . .

I'm not nervous. (I know because I just said it aloud, "I'm not nervous.")

I'm worried about the three or four or five women I don't know suddenly peeing next to th'towel I climax upon. It's hanging two feet from th'head and I'm wondering how their pheromones will . . .

Bukowski. My God and hero and mentor and religious leader, my Job of my own 31 years of scribbling life, BUKOWSKI. They seem to wish to pop a hole in his myth which, according to myself, is not a myth but greater than any fairy tale. After all I studied the man . . . because and only because he selected me.

* * *

133

Twenty-four hours ago a BBC film crew was here. Lights, camera, and action took place.

The shoot went just fine for myself. All the attention was upon me. Someone even put delicious large green fresh ripe seedless grapes in my claw and I nibbled like a King. I was treated like a King . . . for the length of the shoot . . . about one and a half hours. I was paid a couple hundred. They seemed so pleased with my answers and how I comported myself. We all got along so perfectly that I was giddy for a good ten hours after they'd left.

The crew numbered around seven. The director, Vanessa, asked me questions and I answered for the camera. Prior to filming she had told me it would be best for my answers not to acknowledge her questioning because her questions would be edited out.

The crew was sensitive, professional, just fucking terrific. This has me worried. When everything goes in toto right with seven folks working in my cave something has to be fishy. There hasn't been more than two other folks in my cave for a long time.

They began by trying to shake me a bit. They asked me to read a Bukowski poem entitled "300 Poems," his single poem that full-on attacks my odd soul. I asked them if I could first read a Bukowski poem, "Writing," then immediately move into "300 Poems." Vanessa allowed me to do this. She was the boss. I needed $200 and I was not about to be difficult.

Whether or not they filmed myself reading the first poem ("Writing") I don't know but I'm almost certain they did this. Anyhow, the whole recorded and filmed interview, in my opinion, went so well I wondered for the next ten hours or so whether or not I was really having a whipped cream dream. The crew assured me that everything had gone great.

But, the camera "does not lie." And when I finally see the tape, I may well come off onscreen as a hideously vulgar motherfucking asshole. Yesterday was November 28, 1994. I've heard from a close friend "in the know" the finished tape will be out sometime in February, 1995.

There were two women—four or five or more men. I was surprised that fewer women showed up. Maybe I misunderstood.

Vanessa was Director, but she seemed an equal with the soundman, the cameraman, the electrician, the script-girl. And each crew person was from England save for the sound-man, who was born in Kansas.

Well, this recollection has me feeling my prose reads like that of an innocent 53 year old savant, like Dustin Hoffman in "Rain Man."

In fact the crew seemed to coddle me as if I was just this sort of human. They often laughed at my comments. They seemed genuinely amused.

I still feel something was happening that I do not know about. They, especially the script girl (about 35 years old), Elizabeth, didn't want to have any part of the Arrowhead Water I have here. Perhaps a professional film crew has an Ethic: don't nibble from the kitchen of the location's inhabitant.

Perhaps they were a bit puzzled by my interior "decorating."

Perhaps they didn't wish to risk bringing out th'FIEND in me.

I hope they return someday. Viva Bukowski!

# EPILOGUE

A fine sunny clear morn, January 26, 1995, Thursday, about 11 A.M. and birds singing out there as they jerk beaks down to wild birdseed I've spilled from tea-cup purchased at Wednesday's House Coffee House down on Main Street, just about 250 walking yards from this cave.

Crisp, cool, and in toto clean outside. Blue of blues for sky between light pink and flesh toned pillows/puffs of perfect clouds. Beautiful, just perfect upon my eye-ear-cheeks-taste-even smell, and it's the birds still happy chirping, no singing. I love 'em and I love Marissha too, she to my left sitting at table in kitchen, she about nine feet away, quiet and enjoying her peculiar hobby.

Charles Bukowski passed away last March ninth, and now I write *Spinning Off Bukowski.* Chapter by chapter I create what I'm able to recollect of my meetings and interactions with this man who was 20 years older than myself.

For near one month before Marissha arrived I couldn't write any chapters. I was often depressed, stale, sitting on the bed looking down at my very new books: *Hitler Painted Roses, I Am Full of Murder,* and *Stovepiper Book One.* And I felt for whole seconds at a time: these mean nothing. It is all gone. It is useless. I am a pack of playing cards balanced on each other as a house of damn lost cards and now I have collapsed. I am a waste of flesh turned to slop.

Then Marissha came. I've written about a dozen new chapters during her several weeks of living here. "Thank you, dear," I just barely heard myself mutter."

"You have special gifts," say I to Marissha. She's an Aries. Aries can slay. She has Cezanne peach cheeks—best on my eye. I didn't want to live with any woman at all. She overcame my "want." Everytime when she leaves for a walk, I give her a kiss on th'lips (light) because *Blake is absolutely right.* He who kisses a joy as it flies lives in eternity's sunrise.

Once, Bukowski brought a woman here and she was easily the most lovely and attractive woman I had ever seen with him. During the visit he suddenly looked at me and almost whimsically said to her, about me: "He's a bukowski . . . he's a bukowski." Whether or not he truly believed that I was indeed "a bukowski" is something I will never know, and something that doesn't make much difference to me.

Nobody was even close to him, in my opinion, when it came to creating literature.

Not Whitman, nor Ginsberg, nor any of the others on Earth. I hadn't yet read many of them—not Lawrence nor Hamsun nor Bulgakov nor even Dostoevski. But I had read Bukowski in *Ole* magazine and *Wormwood Review* and *Hearse*, and I'd read his *It Catches My Heart in Its Hands* and many other of his collections—*Cold Dogs in the Courtyard, Crucifix in a Deathhand*—and I knew no writer on our planet was near him in guts and passion and intellect too.

All those other great writers were on a highest plateau, but Bukowski was beyond and above them. Bukowski was the life-giving Sun, it seemed to me.

The man who had written the line which goes ". . . the virus holds . . . the concepts give way like rotten shoelace . . ." was here asking to sleep here overnight.

*God, was I blessed . . .* is what I felt that night, over or near 30 years ago.

# INDEX OF NAMES

Artaud, Antonin, 44
Ashbery, John, 19

Baraka, Amiri, 19
Baryshnikov, Mikhail, 76
Baudelaire, Charles, 35, 90
Belli, E.G., 94
Berlinski, Allen, 59, 103
Blackburn, Thomas, 19
Blake, William, 17, 43-44, 137
Blazek, Doug, 96
Bryan, John, 59
Bukowski, Linda Lee Beighle, 112-113, 114-115, 119, 120, 122
Bukowski, Marina, 23, 55, 59, 64, 65, 86
Bulgakov, Mikhail, 138
Bull, Joanna, 73-75
Burroughs, William, 90

Cherkovski, Neeli, 46-48, 49-53, 54, 55, 64, 67-68, 77, 87, 88, 89, 90, 93-95
Coleman, Ornette, 75
Coleman, Wanda, 77-78
Corso, Gregory, 19
Creeley, Robert, 18, 19, 39-40, 44

Dostoevski, Fydor, 138

Ebert, Roger, 9

Elizabeth, 135
Engle, Vanessa, 131, 132-133, 134, 135

Ferlinghetti, Lawrence, 19
Ford, Michael, 82
Frank, Al, 14
Frumkin, Gene, 19, 44

Garcia, David, 103
Genet, Jean, 26, 33
Ginsberg, Allen, 18, 19, 33, 44, 90, 138
Goodwin, Douglas, 103

Hackford, Taylor, 84
Hamsun, Knut, 101, 138
Hemingway, Ernest, 19
Hine, Alvaro Cardona, 19, 44, 55
Hirschman, Jack, 19, 44, 45, 55
Hoffman, Dustin 135

Ives, Charles, 75

Jones, Leroi, 19, 44
Joplin, Scott, 75

K., Nancy Moore, 60-63
Kandel, Lenore, 44
Kandinsky, Wassily, 9
Keats, John, 43
King, Linda, 64, 86, 106, 109, 132

Koertge, Ronald, 81, 82

Lawrence, D.H., 44, 104, 138
"Linda's Sister," 106-107
Locklin, Gerald, 81, 82
Lorca, Garcia, 90
Loren, Sophia, 65

Malley, Stephen, 14, 43-44
Malone, Marvin, 103
Martin, John, 7, 88, 103,
    119-120, 125
McClure, Michael, 19, 44
McDaniel, Wilma, 71
Michelle, Don, 14
Miller, Henry, 15-16, 33
Mondrian, Piet, 9
Monet, Claude, 9
Monk, Thelonius, 75
Morrison, Jim, 93

Norse, Harold, 55, 90-91,
    92-95

Olson, Charles, 19, 39-40, 44

Patchen, Kenneth, 44, 103
Paz, Octavio, 55
Penn, Sean, 128
Perkoff, Stuart, 19
Peters, Robert, 79
Placek, Marissha, 137
Plath, Sylvia, 93, 94, 95
Pleasants, Ben, 81, 82
Pollak, Michael, 59-60
Prevert, Jacques, 44
Purcell, Anna, 16, 60-61,
    63

Richmond, Abraham, 12-13,
    23, 39
Richmond, Denny, 11
Rimbaud, Arthur, 90, 93
Ruby, 43-44

Sam, 131, 132, 133
Sartre, Jean Paul, 26, 33
Schwartz, Max, 12
Shelley, Percy Bysshe, 43
Siskel, Gene, 9
Smith, Frances, 23, 55, 64, 65,
    86
Stockwell, Dean, 85
Stodolsky, Sholom ("Red"),
    128
Stravinsky, Igor, 75
Swallow, Alan, 55

Thomas, Dylan, 19, 44
Thomas, John, 55

Waldron, Daniel, 7-8
Wantling, William, 58
Weinberg, Jeffrey H., 103
Whitman, Walt, 44, 138
Williams, Liza, 64, 109
Williams, William Carlos, 44,
    94
Wordsworth, William, 43

Zahn, Curtis, 41-42

140

Grateful appreciation to the editors of the magazines where various chapters from this book have appeared.

*Atom Mind,* Gregory Smith, editor.

*The Blind Horse Review,* Todd Kalinski, editor.

*Blue Beat Jacket,* Yusuke Keida, editor.

*Bouillabaisse,* Ana & Dave Christy, editors.

*Caffeine Online,* Robert Cohen, editor.

*Chiron Review,* Mike Hathaway, editor.

*pLopLop,* John L. Clark & Kitrell Andis, editors.

*Riot Of The Rats,* David Barker, editor.

*Smellfeast,* Mark Begley, editor.

*Wooden Head,* Mark Hartenbach, editor.

*Wormwood Review,* Marvin Malone, editor.

*Zen Tattoo,* Davd Reeve, editor.